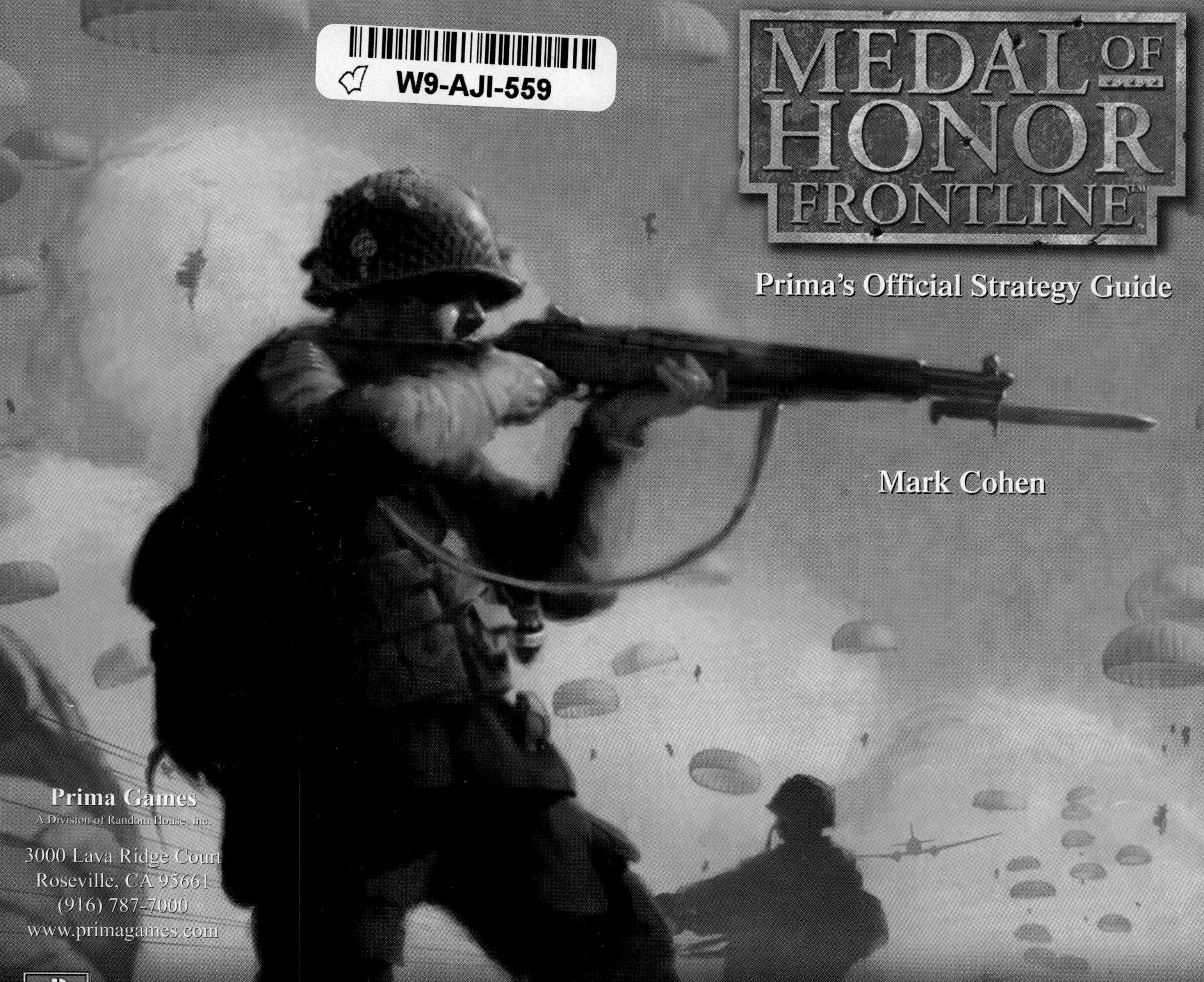

MEDAL OF HONOR FRONTLINE™

Prima's Official Strategy Guide

Mark Cohen

Prima Games
A Division of Random House, Inc.

3000 Lava Ridge Court
Roseville, CA 95661
(916) 787-7000
www.primagames.com

Product Development Manager: Jennifer Crotteau
Associate Product Manager: Christy L. Curtis
Project Editor: Carrie Ponseti
Design & Layout: Bryan Neff, Damon Carlson, Jody Seltzer

ISBN: 0-7615-3767-8
Library of Congress Catalog Card Number: 2002104888
Printed in the United States of America

02 03 04 GG 10 9 8 7 6 5 4 3 2 1

Acknowledgments

A very special thank you to the Electronic Arts Los Angeles creative team, including Scott Langteau and Steve Skelton. *Medal of Honor Frontline* is an exciting and emotional journey, and the artistic genius behind the game is truly inspiring.

I had the privilege of going to war with a battle-hardened Prima Games strike force, led by Product Development Manager Jennifer Crotteau. After landing on the beach, Carrie Ponseti directed the war from her bunker in Roseville. Although our paths did not cross on the battlefield, copy editor Kira Snyder deciphered all of my transmissions with speed and uncompromising accuracy.

Finally, a warrior's tribute to my son Matthew Cohen, who shared my foxhole and led the way on several tough battles. World domination is simply not possible with

CONTENTS

PREPARE FOR YOUR FINEST HOUR

INTRODUCTION

Medal of Honor Frontline takes you to the edge of combat survival in the boots of Lieutenant Jimmy Patterson, a soldier who accepts the reality of war and the challenges it brings. As you move through six missions encompassing 19 levels, you'll experience everything from the pandemonium of landing at Omaha Beach in D-Day to a final confrontation in Stealing the Show. You'll have many important objectives along the way, but your ultimate goal: steal the HO-IX Flying Wing, an experimental Nazi weapon that could spell doom for the Allies.

In every mission you must prove your skills as a "frontline" soldier. This requires you to master more than 20 Allied and German weapons and learn a wide range of strategies and tactics including stealth, hand-to-hand combat, ranged attacks, and demolition. In short, if you want to make it to the victory celebration in one piece, you'll need to walk, run, fire, snipe, strafe, melee, and generally kick butt against hundreds of crack German soldiers who want nothing more than to send you home in a bag.

HOW TO USE THIS GUIDE

This strategy guide contains two parts: Basic Training and The Missions. The first section concentrates on skills such as movement, attack, and specialized operations. *Medal of Honor Frontline* lets you move and fight like a real World War II soldier, so you'll want to master these skills, even if you've done tours of duty on many console battlefields.

After you learn how to control your character, we guide you through exhaustive weapons training. Each weapon in the game not only looks different, but feels unique and possesses different strengths and weaknesses. We pay special attention to range, firepower, mobility, and accuracy. Review this chapter carefully, because your ability to master a specific mission may mean the difference between success and failure in the game.

We also review some of the unusual items and situations you'll encounter in the missions. You face most of the battles alone with your weapon, but many times you must find and use nonaggressive items to meet your objectives.

We conclude Basic Training with the core skills that will help you survive on the battlefield, including short- and long-range tactics, explosives and fixed weapons, and an important tutorial on sniping. In various missions you'll find yourself on both ends of a sniper rifle, and you need to know how to survive.

Already an expert in World War II combat? Skip the first section and report directly to your commanding officer in The Missions. Our walkthroughs take you step-by-step through every objective of every mission, with more than 800 screen shots to help you execute the proper strategies and find your way from point A to point B. Feel free to carve your own path to victory, but consult these "road maps" if you need them.

Enough said. The Higgins boats have started loading and your company needs you on the beach. Good luck, soldier!

CONTROLS

INTRODUCTION

In this chapter we take you through the various options for controlling Lt. Jimmy Patterson. *Medal of Honor Frontline* provides many ways to move and fight, and you'll need to understand each technique to meet your mission objectives.

MOVEMENT

WALK/RUN

This movement uses the pressure sensitivity of the left or right analog sticks. Move the left or right analog stick slightly and Patterson walks; push it to the limit and he runs. You can combine this action with jump.

The fastest way to get Lt. Jimmy Patterson from one place to another: stand and run. Of course, you won't always want to do this, especially if you're moving through enemy-occupied territory. As you travel from one place to another (as opposed to fighting your way through a building or walking through a sniper-infested area), we recommend moving with a rapid-firing, clip-loaded weapon (Thompson SMG, Colt .45, MP-40). This allows you to travel with a fully loaded clip and respond immediately to enemy fire (see the Weapons chapter for recommendations on when to use each weapon).

CROUCH

You crouch by pushing the appropriate button. Patterson can either stand or crouch: he has no in-between state. You can combine this action with walk/run and strafe.

When you can't find adequate cover, crouching presents a much smaller target to the enemy. Furthermore, enemy soldiers must adjust their aim when you go into a crouch, buying you another second or two. You can move into a room unnoticed (at least until you start firing) by crouching as you edge around a corner. What you gain in stealth with crouch, however, you lose in speed. When you need to cover ground quickly, stand up first or your enemies will have the advantage of shooting at a slow-moving crab. In addition to the normal crouching movement, you'll find several situations in the game where you must crouch to fit through an opening or to "see" an object.

STRAFE

Strafe uses pressure sensitivity, even when programmed to a button such as L1 or R1. Push lightly to strafe slowly, or depress the button all the way to strafe at full speed. You can strafe while standing or in a crouch.

Up against multiple enemy soldiers in a small space? Strafe your way out of trouble. Unlike turning, strafe allows you to escape your enemies while inflicting casualties. Strafing works best with a clip-loaded weapon because you don't have the luxury of stopping to readjust your aim.

JUMP

Push the appropriate button to jump; you'll achieve the same height on each jump. You can combine jump with walk/run to leap forward, and you can simultaneously fire and jump.

You might overlook the jump command unless you need it to reach an important location. However, jumping also allows you to see on top of tall objects, where you can often find ammo and health pickups. You can only jump from a standing position.

TURN

You can turn 360 degrees by pushing the left or right analog stick. You can turn when you walk; you do not need to strafe to turn.

CENTER VIEW

Tapping this button instantly brings Patterson's point of view down to a level plane. This is the fastest way to adjust your aim to the horizon after you've lobbed Grenades or aimed at an elevated target.

ATTACKING

FIRE

Push the appropriate button to fire. Press the button once for a single shot; hold the button down for continuous firing (until you've exhausted your ammo). You can combine fire with any of the movement commands described above.

The most basic function of *Medal of Honor Frontline*—shooting a gun—requires no training. You'll kill many of your enemies by shooting them, but remember that firing even one shot instantly reveals your position to the enemy, even if they cannot see you. So avoid shooting an enemy that is in plain view if you can first move to a more desirable (protected) location.

AIM

Pressing the Aim button places a small crosshair on the screen and zooms in at a slightly weaker magnification than the Sniper Zoom (see below). You cannot move while aiming, but you can swing up, down, left, or right.

How you aim depends on whether you require speed or accuracy. You can aim a gun by simply pointing the barrel in the direction of your target and squeezing the trigger. This allows you to keep moving at full speed while firing. However, without the benefit of the crosshair, you compromise your accuracy. By contrast, when you press the Aim button, the target appears closer and the crosshair tells you exactly where the bullet will land. You cannot move forward or backward while you are aiming: you can only raise and lower the gun, or swing it from side to side. While in aim mode, pressing the strafe buttons or up on the left stick allows you to peek around or over obstacles. Releasing the strafe buttons or left stick immediately returns you to your original position. Crouch behind a crate or stand around a corner and you have a great way to take accurate shots without leaving yourself vulnerable to enemy fire.

SNIPER ZOOM

You can only use Sniper Zoom with the Aim button depressed. Only the Springfield Sniper Rifle (Allied) and the Gewehr 43 (German) can use this function. The Sniper Zoom "remembers" your last setting, so if you set it at the highest magnification, the view will remain at this level every time you press the Aim button.

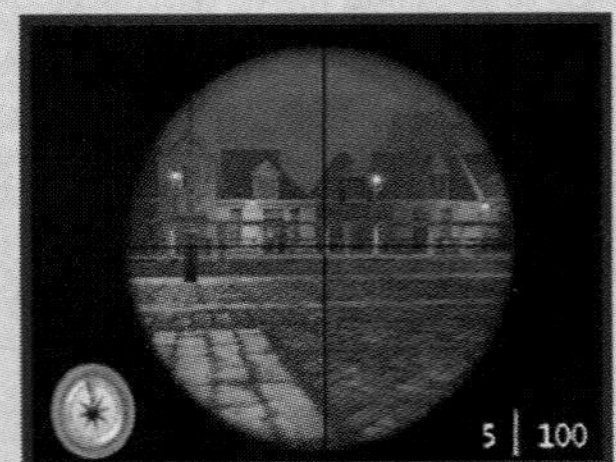

The Sniper Zoom can mean the success or failure of a stealth attack. If you find the right position, you can decimate an entire enemy squad while remaining out of view or out of range. Remember these two weaknesses when using the Sniper Zoom: first, the view disappears while you reload the gun. Second, the gun moves very slowly while using the Sniper Zoom. We recommend pointing your gun in the general direction of the target *before* activating the Sniper Zoom.

MELEE

Every time you push the Melee button, Patterson swings his weapon. In order to connect, locate yourself right next to your target. You can combine melee with any of the movement actions described above. You can also use melee to smash open wooden boxes and the like to locate ammo.

Save melee fighting as a last resort: only a lunatic would charge a machine-gun nest while swinging a rifle. However, there are times when you should use melee rather than fire your weapon, such as when an enemy soldier pummels you with his weapon and is too close for you to quickly and accurately aim your weapon. Also, while you can absorb several hits from the enemy, you can dispatch a German soldier with only one or two blows.

RELOAD

Pressing the Reload button brings the number of bullets in your clip up to the maximum level, with one exception: due to the design of the Garand, you must empty the clip entirely before reloading.

If you have enough ammo, Patterson automatically reloads his weapon when he empties a clip. In normal situations, this works fine; however, we recommend manually reloading whenever possible. This allows you to pick the time and place for reloading, preferably when you are not under direct fire.

AIMING AND THROWING GRENADES

Every time you press the Fire button, Patterson throws a Grenade. The longer you hold the button down, the farther the Grenade travels. Clear out or you will suffer severe damage.

Achieving accurate Grenade tosses depends on aim, trajectory, and strength of throw. You don't have the benefit of a crosshair, so you must look in the direction of your target. You'll find trajectory especially important when you need to toss the Grenade over an object. If you don't raise your point of view high enough, the Grenade will bounce off the object and come right back to you. Finally, strength of throw affects the distance. A quick tap of the Fire button will lob the Grenade only a few feet, a recipe for disaster if you don't run away. Remember to calculate all three factors before tossing a Grenade.

CHANGING WEAPONS

The Next Weapon button cycles through all of your available weapons. Keep in mind that this does not automatically load a weapon, so if you select an empty one, you'll need to manually reload it before you can fire.

OTHER ACTIONS

If you use the classic *Medal of Honor* controller scheme, Action and Reload share the same button. So if you press the Action button with your weapon partially loaded, Patterson will jam in a new clip before completing the desired task.

Lt. Patterson must perform many different tasks other than shooting his weapon. He may set Demo Charges, defuse Dynamite, open doors or secret passages, or start a fire. You complete all of these tasks by pressing the Action button.

WEAPONS

INTRODUCTION

You can't fix a kitchen sink without tools, and you certainly can't fight a war without weapons. In this chapter we examine the weapons available to Lt. Jimmy Patterson in *Medal of Honor Frontline*. Use the Next Weapon button to cycle through your inventory of weapons, most of which you'll carry by hand. The type and number of weapons at the start of each mission may vary, and you can also find weapons during the mission to expand your arsenal. The following list also includes "fixed" weapons that you can fire but not carry.

ALLIED WEAPONS

BANGALORES

Historical Description

Bangalores are long metal pipes generally five feet in length, and each pack several pounds of maximum-yield TNT. You'll find them pushed into the ground below a bunker or infantry obstacle (such as barbed wire), detonated either by remote control or with a fuse delay.

In the Game

Note that only non-playable characters use this weapon. Private Jones uses Bangalores in the first mission of D-Day (Your Finest Hour). You must rescue Jones from an embankment on Omaha Beach and escort him back to the shingle to join your squad. After he arrives, Jones places the Bangalores underneath the barbed-wire entanglement and blows a hole through the obstacle, allowing your squad access to the German bunkers.

BAZOOKA

Historical Description

Early in the war, this antitank rocket launcher weighed 18 pounds and consisted simply of a 54-inch tube open at both ends. A handgrip underneath the tube contained the trigger and electrical contacts that fired a 2.36 inch jet-propelled rocket. The bazooka lacked the punch of the German Panzerschreck, and performed best against targets within 30 yards. Prior to D-Day, the single tube M1A1 evolved to the M9A1, featuring a portable two-part tube and more powerful rocket.

In the Game

When using the Bazooka in *Medal of Honor Frontline*, you must make allowances for the considerable delay between shots. You cannot sit out in the open and repeatedly fire at a target or the enemy will locate and destroy you.

BROWNING AUTOMATIC RIFLE

Historical Description

Commonly referred to as the BAR, this semiautomatic rifle first saw service in World War I. It used a 20-round clip and fired 500 rounds per minute. Hefty at over 18 pounds, the BAR had serious penetrating power; it was Bonnie Parker's (of Bonnie and Clyde) favorite weapon because it could shred police cars.

In the Game

The BAR packs a major wallop. Resist the urge to keep your finger on the trigger, or the 20-shot clips disappear in a hurry.

COLT .45

Historical Description

This semiautomatic pistol performed effectively up to a range of 100 yards. World War II saw the production of more than two million .45's, and the popular Colt had more power and a better service record than the lighter, more finicky German handguns. An older version of the Colt, the model 1917 double-action revolver, found heavy use in North Africa due to the extremely dusty conditions that frequently caused semiautomatic pistols to jam.

In the Game

When you have more powerful weapons at your disposal, you may go several missions without unholstering your Colt .45. But don't sell it short. You'll appreciate the Colt's accuracy, power, and easy aiming. The seven-shot clip lets you hold your own against multiple enemies, and reloading goes quickly.

DEMO CHARGES

Historical Description

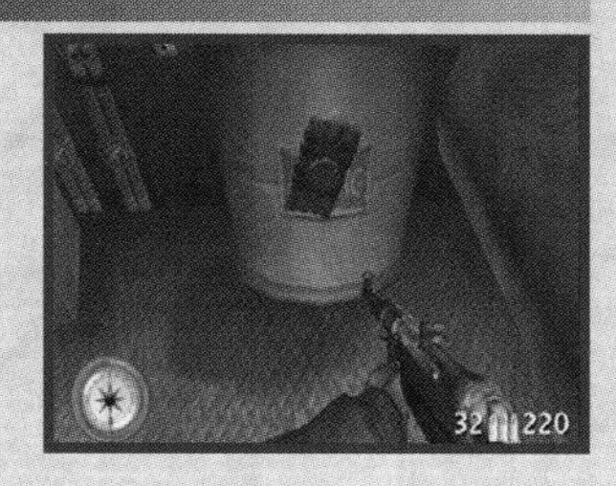

Although Allied engineers routinely used TNT to blow up bridges and buildings, OSS agents and resistance fighters used other, more ingenious explosive devices, such as small pressure-firing triggers used under beds, stairs, and railroad tracks. In 1942, German agents arrived on Long Island, New York, armed with blocks of TNT, fuse coils, and special bombs disguised as large chunks of coal. Fortunately, they aroused the interest of the Coast Guard, who tipped off the FBI, leading to the saboteurs' capture.

In the Game

You'll find Demo Charges easy to use in the game; just remember to clear out before the explosion. Aside from setting charges, you'll also defuse German explosives. You need no special talent or tool; simply get close enough and press the Action button.

M1 GARAND

Historical Description

General George S. Patton called the M1 "the greatest weapon ever made." Designed by John Garand, the M1 fired a .30-06 caliber cartridge in eight-bullet, top-loading clips, and although it weighed nearly 10 pounds, it amazed its users with its dependability and firepower. The U.S. Army used the M1 as a standard issue rifle from 1936 to 1957.

In the Game

Unlike the other semiautomatic weapons in *Medal of Honor Frontline*, the M1 Garand cannot be "topped up" when there are still bullets in the clip. For this reason, you may want to empty a clip completely before walking into a potentially dangerous situation.

MARK II GRENADE

Historical Description

Most GIs could throw a 21-ounce Mark II up to 44 yards. After pulling the pin, a soldier learned to throw the grenade like a baseball. The introduction of the M1 grenade launcher increased the range up to 165 yards.

In the Game

The Mark II Grenade has approximately a three-second delay from throwing it to the time it explodes. Obviously, you'll want to stay clear. One effective tactic: peek around the corner, locate your target, and then bounce the Grenade off the wall without leaving your covered position. Finally, keep in mind that German soldiers love to kick Grenades away or throw them back at you.

SHOTGUN

Historical Description

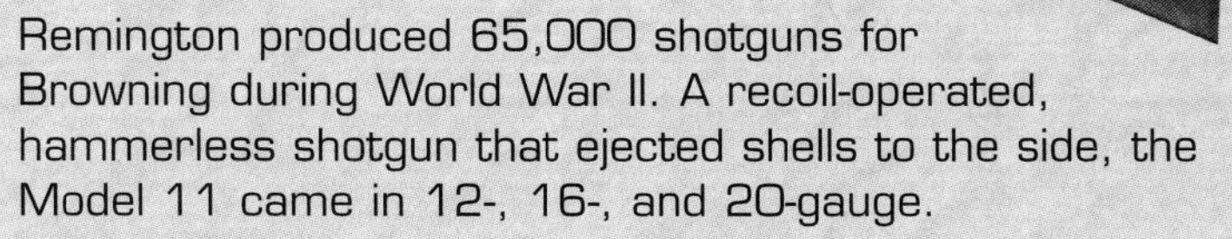

Remington produced 65,000 shotguns for Browning during World War II. A recoil-operated, hammerless shotgun that ejected shells to the side, the Model 11 came in 12-, 16-, and 20-gauge.

In the Game

The shotgun has limited appearances in the game, but you'll welcome it when you face off against several enemy soldiers. Unlike the other guns, you do not have to make a direct hit to inflict injury with a shotgun. However, a single blast from your shotgun rarely kills its intended target, so you may well need to pump and fire again. A shotgun works best at short to medium range.

SILENCED PISTOL

Historical Description

OSS agents during World War II favored the .22 caliber silenced pistol. The addition of a wire mesh baffle to the barrel eliminated the flash and absorbed 90 percent of the noise. William Donovan, Director of the OSS, demonstrated the pistol for President Roosevelt while visiting the White House. Donovan fired ten shots into a sandbag without interrupting the President as he dictated a letter.

In the Game

The Silenced Pistol makes a soft pop when fired—it only alerts enemy soldiers in the immediate vicinity. Similar to the Colt .45, it has a seven-shot clip and displays surprising accuracy and range. You'll want to focus on head shots to conserve ammunition and also lessen the chances for detection.

ALLIED WEAPONS (CONTINUED)

SPRINGFIELD SNIPER RIFLE

Historical Description

Removing the front and rear sights from a stock weapon yielded the .30 caliber Springfield Sniper Rifle. Fitted with a telescopic sight, it outstripped standard issue rifles in accuracy but paled in comparison to the specialized sniper rifles used by the German army. American soldiers did not receive special training as snipers until the Army Marksmanship Unit set up a sniper's school during the Korean War (1954–55).

In the Game

Nothing beats a sniper rifle for decimating a German guard post. If you find excellent cover, you can acquire targets slowly and carefully, with an almost perfect kill rate. Remember that the Springfield carries only five shots in a clip—only half the number in the German Gewehr.

THOMPSON SUBMACHINE GUN

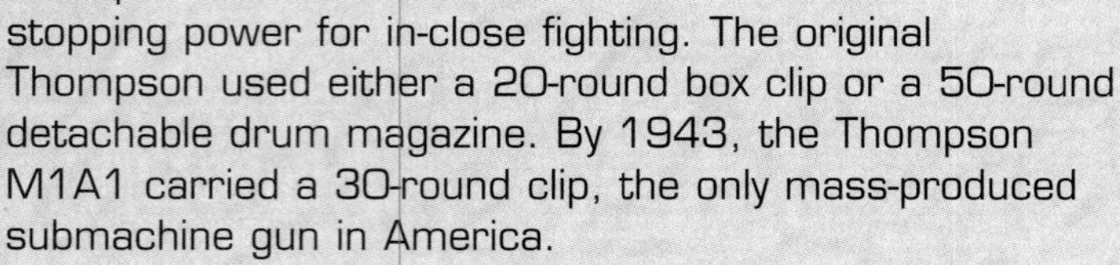

Historical Description

Although heavy (almost 10.5 pounds), soldiers liked the Thompson's rate of fire and stopping power for in-close fighting. The original Thompson used either a 20-round box clip or a 50-round detachable drum magazine. By 1943, the Thompson M1A1 carried a 30-round clip, the only mass-produced submachine gun in America.

In the Game

The Thompson's 20-round clip burns up quickly due to the gun's rapid firing rate, so you can easily blow through your ammo. The gun also has a significant kick, so use it in short bursts where you can re-aim the gun. Finally, you will have better results concentrating on one target at a time rather than spraying bullets as you turn.

GERMAN WEAPONS

GEWEHR 43

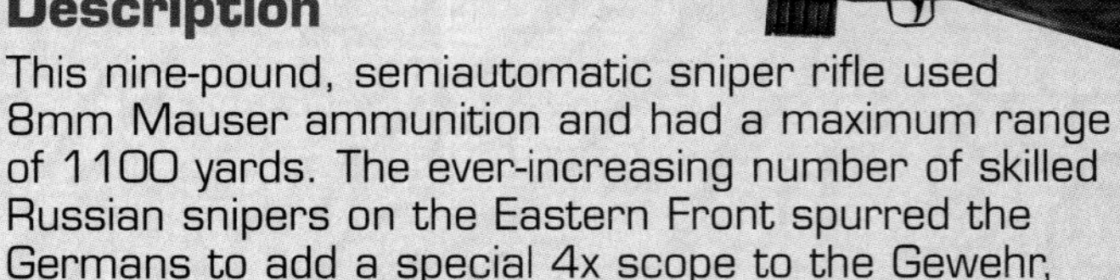

Historical Description

This nine-pound, semiautomatic sniper rifle used 8mm Mauser ammunition and had a maximum range of 1100 yards. The ever-increasing number of skilled Russian snipers on the Eastern Front spurred the Germans to add a special 4x scope to the Gewehr, but production problems limited its distribution.

In The Game

The Gewehr's 10-round clip makes it a more intimidating sniper rifle than the Springfield. Although it lacks the standard crosshairs, you will quickly grow accustomed to the Gewehr sight.

MP-40

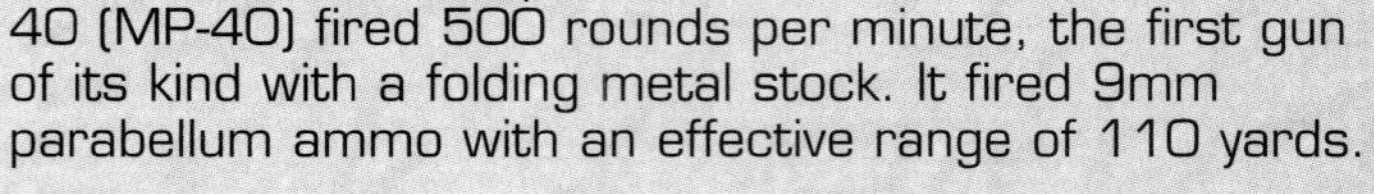

Historical Description

The most famous submachine gun of World War II, the Maschinepistole 40 (MP-40) fired 500 rounds per minute, the first gun of its kind with a folding metal stock. It fired 9mm parabellum ammo with an effective range of 110 yards.

In the Game

The MP-40's 32-round clip makes it a much more productive weapon than the Thompson. The gun kicks up when fired, so aim slightly low for greater accuracy.

MG-42

Historical Description

Nicknamed "Hitler's Buzz Saw," the MG-42 had few if any peers among heavy machine guns. Firing at a blazing 1200–1500 rounds per minute, the MG-42 made a distinctive "zip" sound that terrified Allied troops.

In the Game

When you take over an MG-42 in *Medal of Honor Frontline*, you are king of the hill. For maximum kills, aim low, especially at distant targets. The bullets never run out, so keep your finger on the trigger until you've secured the area. The only downside to manning an MG-42: the limited field of fire, 180 degrees for most guns, so keep your enemy in front of you when manning one of these.

NEBELWURFER

Historical Description

Originally designed to lay down smoke screens, Nebelwurfers soon began service launching rockets that Allied soldiers called "Moaning Minnies." Trucks pulled the early carriage-mounted rocket launchers. The weapon became much more efficient once mounted on a halftrack. Soldiers could fire it and then move it immediately, making it difficult to destroy.

In the Game

You'll have only one opportunity to demonstrate the power of the Nebelwurfer—when you destroy a German tank in the Rough Landing mission. Firing it? Easy. Staying alive long enough to find it? Not.

PANZERSCHRECK

Historical Description

Panzerschreck means "tank terror," and you wouldn't get an argument from an Allied tank commander. Constructed of a lightweight five-foot tube, the Panzerschreck fired a 7.25-pound rocket capable of penetrating 8.25 inches of armor. With a maximum range of 500 feet, the Panzerschreck could pierce the armor of any Allied tank used in World War II.

In the Game

The Panzerschreck wreaks havoc in the game just as it did on the battlefields of World War II. But just like the Bazooka, loading takes time, so find good cover before undertaking a reload.

STEIL GRENADES

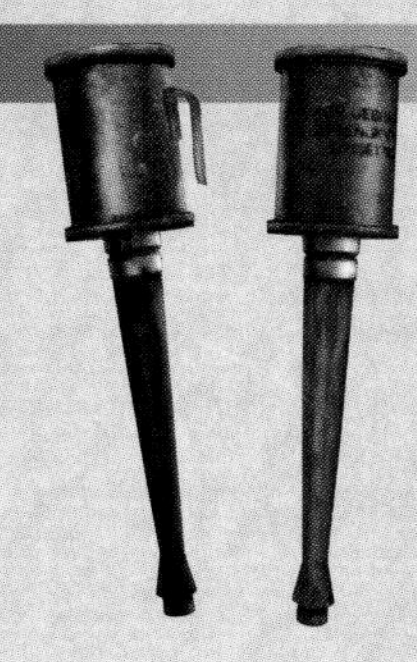

Historical Description

Called the "Potato Masher," the Steilhandgrenate comprised a long wooden handle attached to an explosive can with a pressure-sensitive fuse cap on top. Although the handle made it easy to grasp, personnel found it very cumbersome to carry, so the advantage goes to the Allied Mark II Grenade.

In the Game

The same recommendations hold true for the Steilhandgrenate as for the Mark II. Before you throw one, make sure you measure the strength of your throw, and set proper direction and elevation to reach your target.

STG-44

Historical Description

The world's first assault rifle, the Sturmgewehr MP-44 made its debut in 1942. Equipped with a distinctively curved 30-round box clip, the 44 had an effective range of 330 yards. It fathered the Russian AK-47, still considered the most powerful assault rifle ever made.

In the Game

The STG-44 carries a 30-round clip. Similar in firepower to the BAR, it features more stability, showing very little kick for a gun of its size.

WALTHER P-38

Historical Description

The standard-issue handgun for German officers in World War II, the Walther had a five-inch barrel, fired 9mm parabellum ammo, and had a limited range of 55 yards. The semiautomatic Walther carried an eight-shot magazine.

In the Game

With limited range, the Walther disappoints on versatility. But it still does the trick if you aim well, and when you run out of bullets you can still crack heads with it.

GENERAL TACTICS

INTRODUCTION

Although *Medal of Honor Frontline* is a first-person shooter seen through the eyes of one man, the missions present many opportunities for tactical decisions far beyond simple pointing and shooting. The need for stealth cannot be overemphasized, and the importance of using cover, achieving good sight lines, and staying out of crossfires all contribute to a successful campaign. The mission walkthrough chapters include step-by-step instructions, with tips and strategies for achieving your objectives. But, it always helps to have some basic training before we start using real bullets. The following sections offer general strategies for movement and cover, long-range attacks, short-range attacks, and fixed weapons/explosives.

MOVEMENT AND COVER

Beyond knowing when to walk and when to run, a smart player uses what the battlefield provides. The following list offers tips for staying out of the line of fire as you move toward an objective.

- **Keep moving, soldier!:** Unless you are completely hidden from view on all sides, you should pause the game rather than stand in one spot contemplating the battle. The enemies in this game shoot at anything they can see, so the longer you stay put, the greater your chances of getting hit.
- **When in doubt, crouch:** You cover ground at a snail's pace, but moving in a crouch keeps you alive—especially if you remain out of sight behind a ridge, wall, tree, or other obstacle. Crouching also reveals new pathways under objects such as staircases, vehicles, tables, or rubble. If you don't crouch and examine the surrounding area, you may miss your only escape route or path to the next objective.
- **Pick a side:** If you spend most of your time walking down the middle of the road or across an open pasture, you're tempting the gods of war. Walking alongside a wall, hill, or other obstacle, removes you from a potential enemy sight line.
- **In and out:** To quickly size up what's around the corner or in a room, run out and then immediately step back. As you retreat, watch for gun flashes to identify snipers.
- **Work the perimeter:** It's very intimidating to enter a multilevel room or area with enemies watching you from different elevations. In keeping with our goal to limit the enemy sight lines, start at the highest elevation and clear out the perimeter before you move down to the next level. This limits your exposure while squeezing the enemy into a small, manageable force. This tactic also prevents the enemy from getting behind you, which is the kiss of death on any battlefield.

LONG-RANGE ATTACKS

The Gewehr 43 and Springfield Sniper Rifle are the most effective long-range weapons in *Medal of Honor Frontline*. Each gun lets you zoom in on unsuspecting targets to eliminate them while they patrol, sit, or even sleep. You increase your chances of finishing a mission if you take every opportunity to use a sniper rifle to thin the enemy ranks before you meet them in a close-range attack.

The Mark II Grenade and Steil Grenades are often overlooked as long-range weapons. They are especially effective for attacking around a corner (using a ricochet throw) or over a tall obstacle. However, unlike the sniper's bullet, an enemy soldier can spot a flying grenade and kick it away—or throw it back at you! A grenade is also an excellent diversion. The explosion is a distraction, allowing you to move unseen through a dangerous area. Finally, a grenade is effective for getting one or more enemies to change locations. For example, a group of soldiers waiting in ambush around a corner will usually run for cover when a grenade comes over the wall. An alert soldier will move up quickly, take the covered position, then use it against the enemies.

SHORT-RANGE ATTACKS

A melee attack sounds exciting, but unless the circumstances are ideal, it spells disaster. True, it only takes two swings to kill an enemy soldier, but unless you have the element of complete surprise, most enemy soldiers respond with something much more damaging than the butt of a gun. Save melee attacks for situations where you can silently sneak up on a target and effect a quick kill. An even better use of melee is to smash a box to reveal ammo or health pickups inside. This saves valuable ammo and it is much quieter.

In general, the shorter the barrel, the better a weapon is at short-range attacks. Hence, a sniper rifle and a bazooka do not fair as well as a Colt .45 or an MP-40. When fighting at close range, shoot quickly and move even faster. This leaves little time for using the aiming crosshairs. A short-range attack is even more effective when combined with a strafing move, where a soldier runs sideways while firing. This is a great way to take out enemy soldiers when they are bunched together.

EXPLOSIVES AND FIXED WEAPONS

There is only one strategy for using explosives: run away! Standing around to admire your handiwork will only result in your health being reduced by about 50 percent. Unfortunately, you cannot randomly use explosives in the game. Instead, each location for planting an explosive charge is outlined in the mission.

A fixed weapon, as the name suggests, is a weapon that cannot be moved. In the game, this includes the following:

- **U-Boat Deck Gun**
- **Nebelwurfer**
- **Panzer IV Turret Gun**
- **MG-42**

The most productive of these weapons is undoubtedly the MG-42. After you clear out the enemy gunners, you can take over the gun at any time, and the ammo never runs out. The MG-42 is devastating when aimed low and raked across a group of soldiers. However, the sheer power of the MG-42 can lull you into thinking you are invulnerable. On the contrary, you are visible to the enemy, and you are in a fixed position. Hence, you should limit your time behind the trigger, especially if you are receiving fire from several directions.

D-DAY

YOUR FINEST HOUR

MISSION OBJECTIVES

- Meet the Captain on Shore
- Rescue Four Pinned-Down Squad Members
- Rejoin Squad at Shingle Embankment
- Rescue Engineer at End of Embankment
- Rendezvous with Captain at Base of Bunker
- Cross the Minefield and Man Machine Gun
- Destroy MG Nests on Ridge

WEAPONS

- Colt .45
- M1 Garand
- Thompson SMG

NOTE – Remember, when you land at Omaha Beach you are facing *South*.

MEET THE CAPTAIN ON SHORE

The trip to the shore in a Higgins boat makes you seasick and apprehensive for what awaits you on the beach. As the door falls open to the surf, an explosion blows you clear of the craft, and you begin the mission underwater, watching your buddies struggle to the surface. Some make it, but many do not. Your feet touch bottom, and you can run for the sand. Along the shoreline and to the left of your opening position is the Captain, waving and calling to you from behind a beached Higgins. Run to him; crouch behind him, away from enemy fire. Listen to his commands, but keep your head down, or you'll take some hits before you hit the beach.

RESCUE FOUR PINNED-DOWN SQUAD MEMBERS

The Captain's orders: Find and aid four squad members who are scattered across the beach, trapped by enemy fire. Provide enough cover fire for each soldier to leave his position and move toward the shingle (an area along the seawall blocked by barbed wire). Each of the four soldiers will wave and call out as you approach, but you may find it difficult to hear or see this in the noise and pandemonium of the beach. Collect Medicinal Canteens or other health packs to stay alive. As you rescue each soldier, remember that you must direct cover fire at one of the two bunkers, as described below.

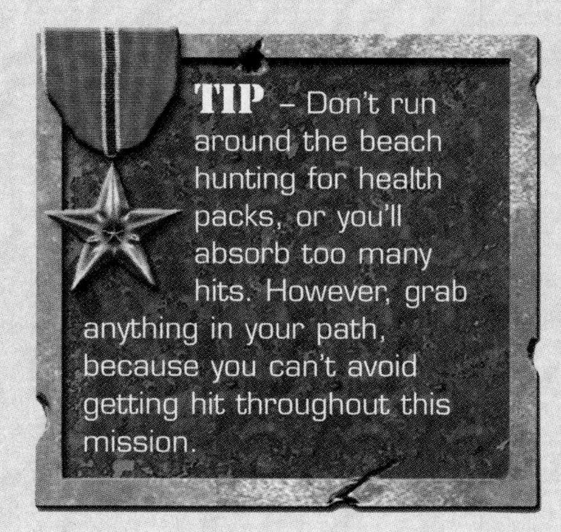

TIP – Don't run around the beach hunting for health packs, or you'll absorb too many hits. However, grab anything in your path, because you can't avoid getting hit throughout this mission.

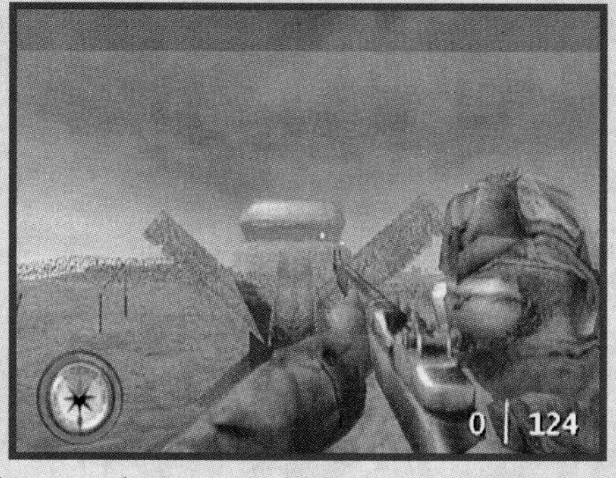

Begin your search along the waterline to the west. When you reach a position in front of the right-hand bunker, find the soldier hiding behind an obstacle. Approach his position and crouch down immediately, taking aim at the southeast bunker. Fire into the dark area, the source of the enemy fire. Keep firing. The explosions knock your gun all over the place, so remember to re-center your gun on the target. After several good shots, your squad mate will take off toward the seawall. Three more to go.

Return to the waterline where you take cover behind the obstacles as you move slightly farther to the west. Keep your eyes on the sand just beyond the water, and you see a soldier kneeling behind an obstacle. Wait for an opening in the enemy fire, and run to the soldier. Crouch down and find a position where you can fire at the southwest bunker without taking too much damage.

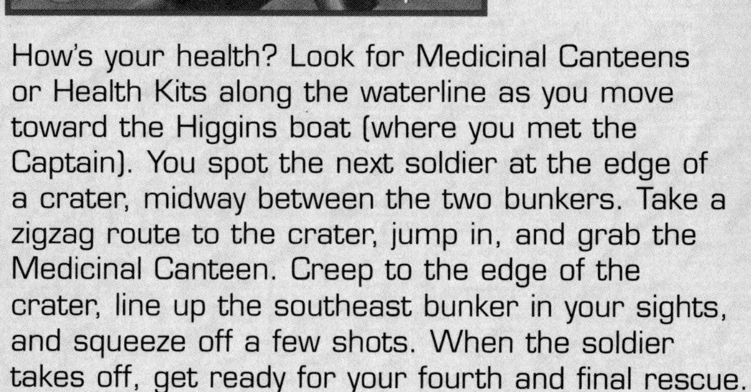

How's your health? Look for Medicinal Canteens or Health Kits along the waterline as you move toward the Higgins boat (where you met the Captain). You spot the next soldier at the edge of a crater, midway between the two bunkers. Take a zigzag route to the crater, jump in, and grab the Medicinal Canteen. Creep to the edge of the crater, line up the southeast bunker in your sights, and squeeze off a few shots. When the soldier takes off, get ready for your fourth and final rescue.

REJOIN SQUAD AT SHINGLE EMBANKMENT

Return to the previous obstacle (where you found the second soldier), and look to the southeast where the last soldier sits trapped behind another obstacle, close to the shingle. You'll find an M1 ammo pack along the way. After laying down cover fire on the southeast bunker and releasing the soldier, run to the shingle to meet your squad. Wait, however, until the German fighter passes overhead, or you might run into a strafing line of .50 caliber bullets.

When you reach the shingle, you see the Captain, surrounded by the four soldiers you rescued. He directs one of the soldiers to go find the Bangalore Torpedo engineer. Alas, enemy fire cuts him down before he takes ten paces down the beach. Now it's up to you. Crouch down and head west behind the shingle. Resist the temptation to stand up and run, or you'll get shredded.

RESCUE ENGINEER AT END OF EMBANKMENT

When you reach the end of the beach, you see the engineer, Private Jones, crouched behind a wedge-shaped metal frame. Pick up the Thompson SMG lying in the sand at the rear of the wedge. Jones tells you to lay cover fire on the southeast bunker. When he takes off, keep your head down and follow him back to the shingle.

RENDEZVOUS WITH CAPTAIN AT BASE OF BUNKER

If you can see this much of the explosion, you're much too close!

TIP – As you approach the bunker, pick up the Field Surgeon Pack and Thompson ammo to the left of the Captain.

When Jones sets his charge, move away from the blast area to avoid taking damage. When the seawall clears, the Captain sees a defilade position (protection from enemy sight line and fire). You receive orders to move quickly with the rest of the squad to the base of the southeast bunker.

CROSS THE MINEFIELD AND MAN THE MACHINE GUN

Negotiate the minefield as you scurry to an unmanned, mounted machine gun at the far western end of the trenches. Mines blow up all around (and under) you, but don't slow down. Move quickly, running from crater to crater to avoid the mines, and enter the trenches through a blast hole in the wall. German soldiers might peek around the corner ahead, but don't engage them, at least not until you wrap your fingers around the MG-42. Turn right, take out the lone German soldier blocking your path, and climb the ladder to the machine gun.

DESTROY MG NESTS ON RIDGE

When you get up to the MG-42, press the Action button to take control of the weapon, and level the German soldiers moving down the trench toward you. When you've finished them off, train the gun on the two machine-gun nests between the bunkers. The one on the right quickly goes up in smoke, but cleaning out the left-hand nest takes time. Several German soldiers reinforce the position; keep firing until the nest explodes into a cloud of smoke.

Climb down from the gun, and return to the trench where your Captain waits. He congratulates you for a job well done, and you turn to face the steel door that opens into the bunkers. You survived the landing on Omaha Beach! Now comes the hard part.

NOTE – You do not need to eliminate the German soldiers and destroy the machine-gun nests in any particular order. You may have better luck killing the first group of soldiers in the trench and then turning the guns briefly on the machine-gun nests before finishing off the remaining soldiers.

INTO THE BREACH

MISSION OBJECTIVES

- Clear Machine-Gun Bunker
- Destroy Radio Link to Upper Gun Deck
- Find Smoke Grenades
- Clear Both Gun Decks
- Mark Gun Deck with Smoke Grenade

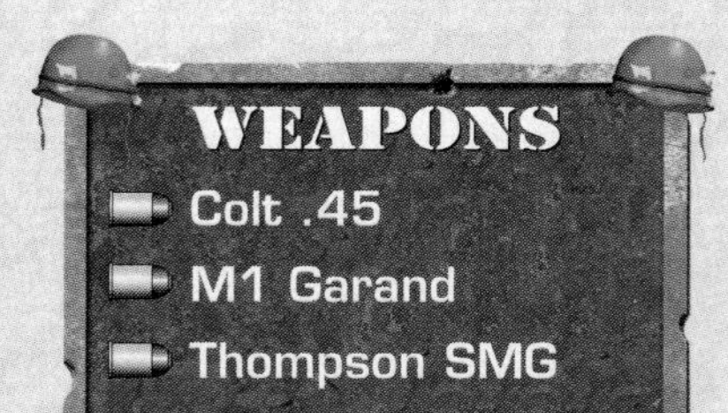

You neutralized a substantial number of enemy troops on your way to the bunker door, but D-Day holds more challenges for you. Fight your way to the top of the bunker, and place a Smoke Grenade so the flyboys can reduce the bunker to rubble. At the end of the last mission, the bunker door was closed. In this mission, the door is open, and the German soldiers on the other side are laying down fire—proceed with care.

CLEAR MACHINE-GUN BUNKER

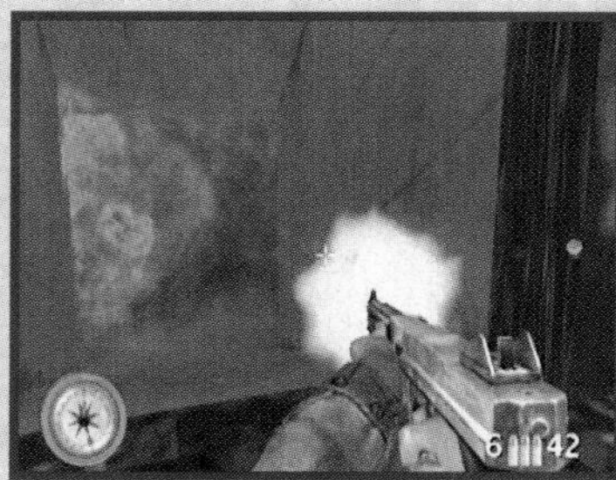

A ramp leads from the door down to a lower level, where an MG-42 peppers the entrance with heavy fire from behind a tiny window. Crouch down and inch your way around the corner of the trench until you have a shot at the window. Or, race out and shoot the gasoline barrels at the bottom of the ramp for a nice big bang that takes out the gunner.

With the machine gun silenced, load a fresh clip in the Thompson and move down the ramp. Turn left and proceed down the corridor, stopping to pick up the Field Surgeon Pack. At the end of the corridor, crouch and inch your way around to the right until you see the fuel barrels against the wall. Blow them up to destroy the German soldier hiding around the corner. After the blast, move around the corner to finish off the enemy (if he still lives). Another soldier may step out of the room to the right of the stairway, so don't stop too long.

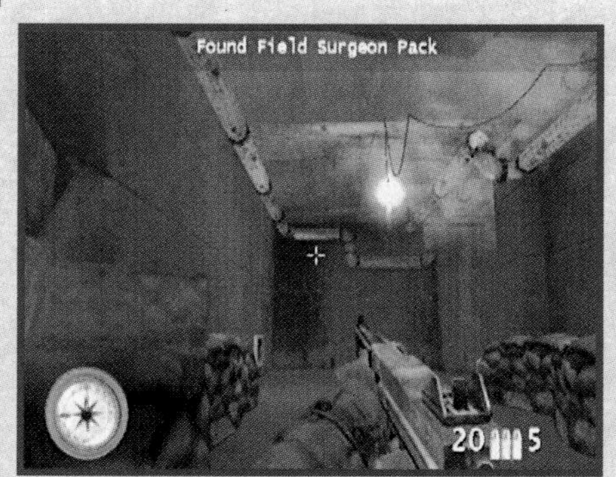

Continue carefully around the corner to the right; you encounter another soldier or two still in the room. Don't wait for the soldier to pop up from his hiding place—blast through the barrels for a quick kill. Grab the cache of Thompson and Garand ammo in the crates, reload, and move slowly around the corner to the MG-42 room.

CAUTION – Although you took out the gunner from the top of the ramp, his buddy lurks in wait for you, hiding behind his dead comrade. He starts firing with a submachine gun as soon as you poke your head around the corner, so make sure you take him out! When you kill the second gunner, you've officially cleared the Machine-Gun Bunker.

DESTROY RADIO LINK TO UPPER GUN DECK

After clearing the room, take control of the MG-42 and look out the window. Several German soldiers reenter the trench, and with the remainder of your squad working their way through the other bunker, you have no one to watch your back. Eliminate all four soldiers here (the last one drops down from the trench wall after a brief delay), or they will attack you from behind when you enter the stairway.

Reload your Thompson before leaving the room, because you encounter one or two Germans before you reach the stairway (depending on how many you have already killed). The first landing poses no problems, but you run across a guard on the next landing, so don't bolt up the stairs. Instead, crouch down, inch around the corner, and target the German soldier from a position on the landing below. Race up the stairs in time to see him hit the ground.

On the third landing, a soldier frantically radios a message to the upper part of the bunker (the message appears on your screen). Bear to the right and follow the wall until you reach the radio room; a lone soldier is at the microphone. Shoot him in the back and then destroy the radio link.

FIND SMOKE GRENADES

Now you must find the Smoke Grenades, but you'll need to fight your way through heavy resistance. Leave the radio room, crouching down as you hug the wall, continuing to the right. A German soldier hears you coming and flips a table over for cover, making him a difficult target. Rather than try for a head shot, blow up the small fuel barrel to the left of the table. Stay in your crouch and turn toward the back of the room, where another machine-gun-toting soldier is waiting.

Run to the metal shelves and take cover behind the stack of lumber. This protects you from the soldier firing from behind the open door to the left. If you hang around in the middle of the room, you'll take serious damage. By now your Thompson ammo is probably low, so switch to your Colt .45 or M1 Garand. After a few seconds behind the woodpile, remain in your crouch and move forward. Take it slow and easy, and you'll have a good shot as you approach the door. Take the enemy out and proceed into the room. Climb the ladder, but first jump up onto the wooden crates to grab the Field Surgeon Pack.

Take the ladder all the way to the top (you automatically jump off the ladder when you reach the ceiling). The explosions come more frequently now, and as you step off the ladder you hear coughing from the next room. Move through the doorway and shoot the distracted German soldier sitting on the floor. Move through the next doorway and around the corner, but avoid the ladder—it doesn't go anywhere. Furthermore, if you stop to check it out, a German soldier tosses a Grenade from the other room, and you'll take a serious health hit.

When the dust settles, proceed into the next room and hug the right-hand wall. Turn the corner; a German soldier fumbles for his weapon. Shoot him before he gets off a shot and then collect the cache of M1 and Thompson ammo in the room.

As you enter the tunnel, you see a crate of Smoke Grenades. Grab them and then train your sights on the support beams straight ahead—a German soldier's hiding place. Take him out and move to the next set of support beams where another soldier waits to ambush you. Continue winding through the tunnel until you reach a doorway.

Large wooden crates fill this room, and the enemy soldiers here have excellent cover. Crouch down and advance carefully, behind the cover of the crates. When you reach the crates, pop up and strafe left and right to take care of the two soldiers. Go back into your crouch. Weave your way around the boxes to the other end of the room where a doorway leads you back into the tunnel. At least one German soldier lurks near the doorway.

Continue through the tunnel, where you encounter another elusive enemy soldier. Take him out with the first shot, or he'll retreat and hide behind the timbers. When you reach the next room, crouch down and work your way around the crates, moving to the left. As you round the corner, you see two German soldiers with weapons drawn. Shoot the fuel barrels to toast both soldiers.

A doorway leads back into the tunnel. You receive fire when you step into the short corridor beyond the doorway—two German soldiers hide in the next room, one behind an overturned table. A tough shot, no question. Find a good angle and try to avoid being in the line of fire for too long. After clearing the last soldier, walk past the overturned table and gather the health pickups and Thompson ammo in the alcove down the hall.

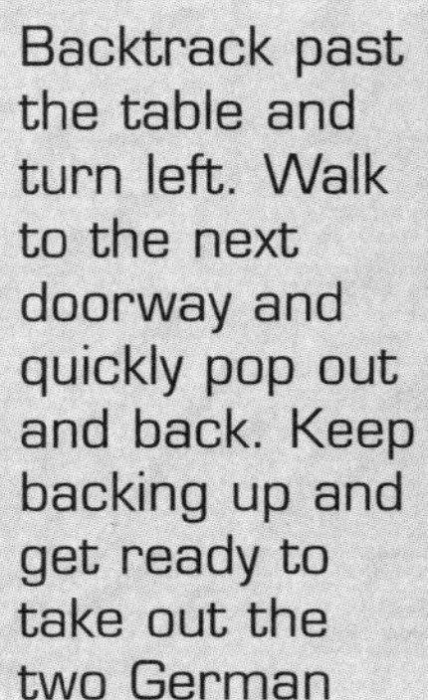

Backtrack past the table and turn left. Walk to the next doorway and quickly pop out and back. Keep backing up and get ready to take out the two German soldiers who fill the doorway. Reload, crouch down and inch around the left side of the doorway until you see the enemy soldier firing at you from behind a stack of boxes. Take him out, refresh your health with the Field Surgeon Pack and then proceed past the boxes to another doorway that leads to a ladder. Note a blue metal door at the other end of the hallway; you cannot open it, so don't waste your time.

You hear machine-gun fire resounding from the gun deck. Climb to the top of the ladder and walk into the adjacent room, where a German soldier waits for a radio message that he will never receive (thanks to you!). Take him out and proceed to the metal door that leads to the gun deck.

CLEAR BOTH GUN DECKS

Deafened by the noise on the deck, the German soldiers do not turn around until you start firing. The Thompson works best here, and if you've conserved your ammo, you should have enough to clear the deck. If you run out, use the M1 Garand, but since you cannot spray fire from side to side, the need for single-shot accuracy dramatically increases.

After you've cleared the deck, keep your eyes on the second deck. American planes dive in and strafe it, killing the enemy gunners. The Captain appears on the second deck, waves to you, and then sets Smoke Grenades for the planes to target. They return and bomb the second bunker, putting it permanently out of commission.

MARK GUN DECK WITH SMOKE GRENADE

It's your turn. A flashing red square appears at the center of the deck. Move close to the square and use the Action button to place the Grenades. The attack comes quickly, so clear the deck or you'll go up with it. Turn around, make a hard left, and head for the back entrance to the trenches. After the explosion, continue down the trenches and meet up with the Captain who congratulates you on another excellent mission. Thanks to you, Omaha Beach is secure!

A STORM IN THE PORT

SEASIDE STOWAWAY

MISSION OBJECTIVES

- Collect Resistance Drop at Insertion Point
- Man Machine Gun in Church Tower
- Secure Submarine Fueling Roster
- Breach Wall to Docks
- Locate Submarine Fueling Dock
- Stowaway in Cargo Crate

WEAPONS

- Colt .45
- M1 Garand
- Mark II Grenades

COLLECT RESISTANCE DROP AT INSERTION POINT

Your mission begins in a small clearing surrounded by trees. From your opening position, you see a small white object behind a cluster of wooden crates: the Resistance Drop. Approach the item, press the Action button to retrieve it and then proceed down the path to your left.

MAN MACHINE GUN IN CHURCH TOWER

Don't get overconfident just because you aced the first objective. Several obstacles, both human and mechanical, stand between you and the church tower. As you near the end of the path, a jeep barrels down the road in front of you, moving from right to left. Ignore the gunfire; you won't get hit. Chase the jeep as it continues down the road, and get as close as possible to the passenger side when it overturns. The injured driver implores you to take over the machine gun. Do this quickly by moving next to the gun and pressing the Action button.

Across the courtyard there are three or four German soldiers peppering your squad mates. At least one soldier lurks behind the sandbags in the center of the screen as three or four pour out of the building on the right. Another will appear shortly in the archway on the left. The machine gun lacks the accuracy of your M1. Aim low and sweep back and forth, taking care not to hit your own men as they move in front of you. Clear the building on the right, because you need to gather supplies there after you leave the jeep.

Clear the courtyard and enter the aforementioned building; pick up the ammo caches and Field Surgeon Pack (if your health is less than 100 percent). If you're in perfect shape now, come back later when you need a major health boost. The fight continues down the street, but don't leave until you scour the courtyard and passageways for an assortment of ammo and Grenades.

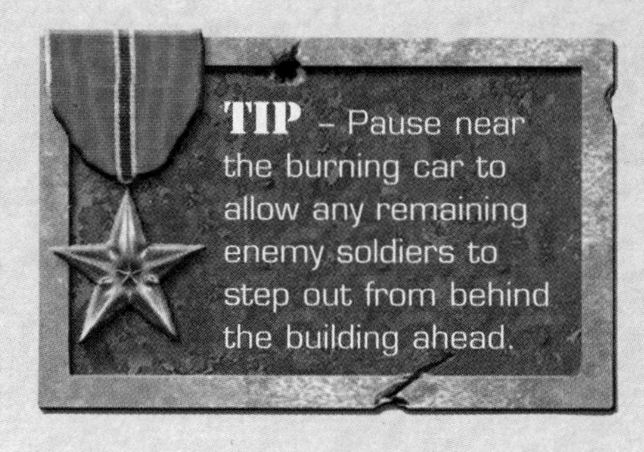

TIP – Pause near the burning car to allow any remaining enemy soldiers to step out from behind the building ahead.

Move down the right side of the street, taking cover at the side of the building. A German soldier lurks behind the building on the left near a burning car and another on the same side, farther up the street. Edge out for a good shot, but don't take unnecessary chances, because within moments a friendly plane drops a well-placed bomb and turns him to dust. Watch for more enemy fire on the right side of the street. When you see your chance, sprint to the burning car where you find some ammo and a Medicinal Canteen.

At first glance, the street looks clear to the north, and you see two Medicinal Canteens down a narrow alleyway. However, up to four German soldiers wait to ambush you from the alleyway on the left. Crouch down, approach slowly, and get ready to take them out. If you'd rather kill them from afar, step out just far enough to bounce a Grenade off the far wall. Pick off the ones trying to escape the blast.

After picking up the Canteens, return to the passageway and follow it to the end, where you find another Medicinal Canteen. Crouch down and crawl through the jagged opening on your left, then leave the building and walk up the cobblestone street. As you approach the street, you see machine-gun tracers from a German tank firing from across the bridge to your right. You must get past the tank in order to blow it up and reach the church tower, but this takes careful planning.

Note the Medical Kit at the corner of the building. Danger awaits you out in the street, but if your health looks grim, grab the kit now, before you tangle with the tank. Run full speed, dodging back and forth until you reach the burned-out car up ahead on the left. Crouch down behind the rear bumper. Check your weapon and then pop up to target the German soldiers on the other side of the river: one in a bunker and the other moving back and forth.

Race across the street (you can't afford to crouch or take your cautious time here) and down the passageway on the right side of the building. From a crouch, turn left at the end of the building and inch your way toward the river. Train your M1 on the fence on the other side of the river. Use the low wall for cover, and fire at the two German soldiers on the other side. With enemy infantry eliminated on either side of the bridge, nothing stands between you and that tank.

Return to the edge of the building that faces the main street. If you need a health boost, run inside the building to grab the Medical Kit, but move quickly—you don't want to test the tank's accuracy from inside its line of sight. Wait until the turret moves away from your position, then race across the bridge and duck into the building behind and to the right of the tank, where you find a Medicinal Canteen and some ammo. Peek around the corner and wait until the gun turret faces the bridge. When it's clear, step out from behind the tank and lob three Grenades at the turret. Check out the surrounding buildings and passageways for ammo and health packs. With full health and plenty of bullets, concentrate on reaching the church tower.

Run down the street past the tank and enter the bombed-out remains of the church. An injured radioman is on the left, and an urgent message orders you up to the gun in the tower. Use the Action button to attach yourself to the ladder on the left and then scurry to the top of the tower (look up, then walk with the D-Pad). When you reach the top, you will automatically let go of the ladder.

Take control of the MG-42 on the ledge, and destroy the German soldiers gathering in the street and in the building on the left. Don't abandon the gun until you kill them all.

SECURE SUBMARINE FUELING ROSTER

Climb down the church tower ladder (press the Jump button when you reach the bottom). Grab the Field Surgeon Pack if you need it. Exit the courtyard, but watch for a German soldier hiding under the archway across the street and to the left.

Your next objective is down the street to the right, but you can exit the church and turn left if you need to forage for medical supplies or ammo. Watch out for the two German soldiers hiding in the passageway on the left. If you receive fire from behind, spin around and take out the German soldier in the brick-enclosed yard across the street. Gather a Medical Kit and ammo in the room at the end of the passageway, and run back across the street to pick up another Medicinal Canteen in the yard, if you need it.

Go back past the church (turn right if you are exiting the church). Keep alert for the two German soldiers ahead, one is in the doorway of a bombed-out building on the left, and the other is at the intersection on the right. Dispatch both soldiers, then pick up the Medicinal Canteen at the end of the street.

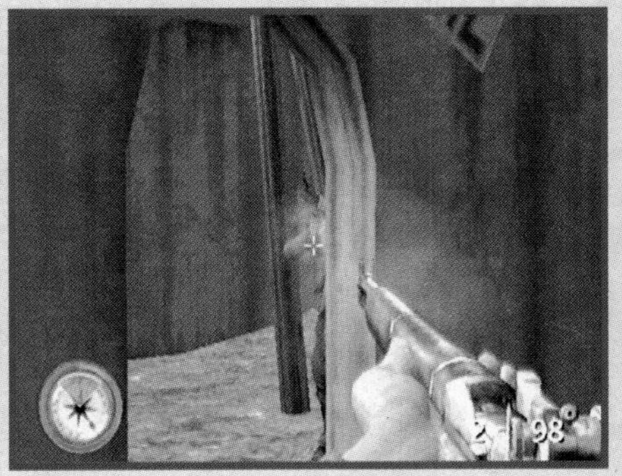

After retrieving the Canteen, enter the large doorway that leads into a warehouse. Once inside, you see crisscrossed timbers that block access to an enemy-occupied courtyard. If you crouch down and advance slowly, you can take out two unsuspecting German soldiers. Another soldier enters the courtyard from the right, and still another steps out from a warehouse. You can easily take them all. Eliminating as many Germans as possible from this position makes your upcoming entry into the courtyard easier.

The downside to this little courtyard frolic: if any of the German soldiers escape, they'll wait for you to crawl through the opening on the left. So, crouch down and move forward just far enough to target a soldier who might take a shot at you from the other room. When you can, crawl through the opening, pick up the Medicinal Canteens, and enter the courtyard to the right.

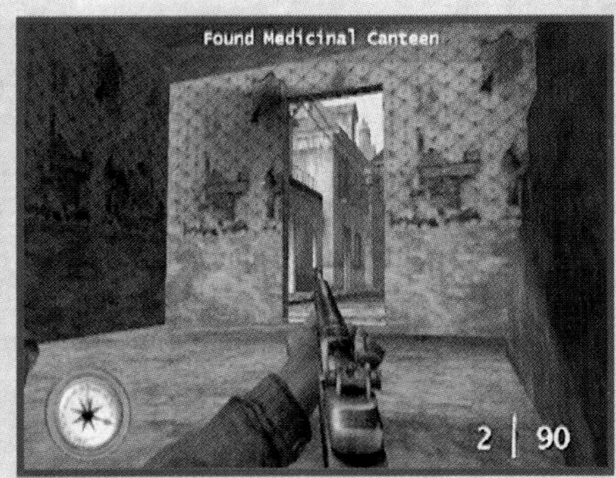

Although you took out several soldiers, one or two are still hanging around. One of your buddies arrives to help you finish the job. After you clear the courtyard, pick up the scattered ammo and medical supplies; remember to check the warehouse directly across the courtyard. Turn right and exit the courtyard through the passageway that takes you back to the street.

Cross the street and walk through the large opening. A Medical Kit is in the corner on the right, and a German officer interrogates an American soldier. Crouch down and enter the jagged hole in the wall straight ahead. The low ceiling requires you to stay in a crouch as you make your way to the left. You cannot save the American soldier from execution, but when you arrive at the opening to the room, take revenge on the German officer. He's an easy mark with his back turned, but don't dawdle. He will eventually turn around and start firing. Collect the Fueling Roster from the wall and take the ammo and Medicinal Canteen.

BREACH WALL TO DOCKS

TIP – Throw the Grenade immediately, or the enemy soldiers will run toward you with guns blazing. If this happens, retreat back into the room, go into a crouch, and squeeze off several shots as the soldiers gather in the street just outside the door. When you emerge again, three more soldiers take over the machine gun. This time, quickly throw your Grenade.

Now you have what you need to complete this mission, but you'll need to take out several more enemies before your job is done. Before walking back onto the street, arm yourself with a Grenade, and turn to your right as you exit. Toss the Grenade to take out the German soldiers manning the MG-42 bunker.

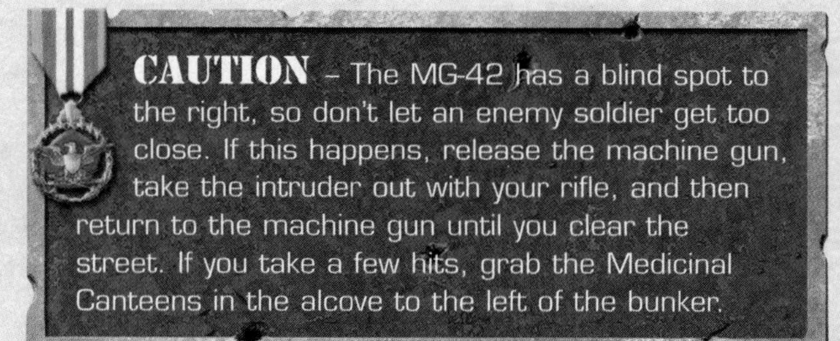

CAUTION – The MG-42 has a blind spot to the right, so don't let an enemy soldier get too close. If this happens, release the machine gun, take the intruder out with your rifle, and then return to the machine gun until you clear the street. If you take a few hits, grab the Medicinal Canteens in the alcove to the left of the bunker.

The sound of the explosion alerts more German soldiers, but you have time to grab the MG-42 and spray the street with bullets as the soldiers spill onto the street (watch out for your squad mates as they advance up the street in your line of fire). Despite your heavy weapon, the enemy can get you in their crosshairs, so keep firing until all of the gray uniforms go down.

With the street clear, walk a few paces forward and turn to your left; there are several fuel drums positioned in front of a stone wall. A few well-placed rifle shots will ignite the fuel and blast a hole in the wall. Take your time here, especially if you need to increase your health. Before blasting the wall, continue down the street and collect the Medicinal Canteens behind the bunker. Farther ahead you find Grenades in the corridor on the left and a Medical Kit in the alley on the right. Now you should be back to full strength and well armed with Grenades. You'll need both for the upcoming fight.

LOCATE SUBMARINE FUELING DOCK

Step through the rubble of the wall and turn right. Proceed until you see a German sentry. Take him out, run down the path, and take over the MG-42 on the right. Target the soldiers at the MG-42 nest down the road. When nothing stirs, release the gun and proceed to the submarine fueling dock.

NOTE – Another path through the trees takes you directly to the Submarine Fueling Dock, but you must fight your way through the guards with just your field weapons. Your chances are better if you use the machine gun, eliminate the German soldiers from afar, and then walk to the dock.

STOWAWAY IN CARGO CRATE

You're almost home. Find the open crate among the cluster of wooden boxes—this is your ride to the next mission. Crawl into the crate, and pat yourself on the back for a job well done.

SPECIAL CARGO

MISSION OBJECTIVES

- Sabotage U-Boat Engines
- Set Explosives in Aft Torpedo Room
- Disable Radio Communications
- Set Explosives in Fore Torpedo Room and Find Enigma Code Book
- Escape through Exit Hatch

WEAPONS

- Colt .45
- MP-40
- Explosives

SABOTAGE U-BOAT ENGINES

You begin this mission inside the same crate you jumped in at the end of Seaside Stowaway. Aim your .45 at one of the two sailors in front of you, and press the Action button to open the crate. Both sailors pull their weapons when they hear the noise; take them out. Crouch behind the crate, and crawl to the right where you find three 64-round MP-40 ammo boxes. Return to your original position, move forward, and grab the ammo and MP-40 machine pistol on the box to your left (blue rectangle). You'll need every bullet for this mission, so take everything.

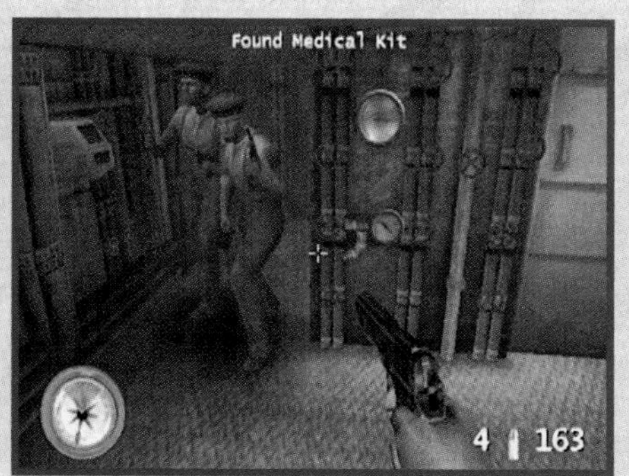

Open the door directly in front of you, take a couple steps forward, and swing to your right to kill a seaman as he attempts to fire his pistol from the bathroom. Pick up the dropped ammo and expect more company when you exit the bathroom. Two seamen leave the lounge and come after you. Return fire if they attack, but don't chase them just yet. Instead, open the gray metal door to the right and collect the Medical Kit and lots of ammo for your MP-40.

Continue down the hallway with the red glow, and get ready to shoot the three or four sailors relaxing in the eating quarters. Pay special attention to a machine-gun-toting soldier who pops up from behind the last booth on the left.

When you reach the end of the eating area, a chef heaves cleavers at you from the galley. Stay to the right to avoid the blades, and pick up the Medicinal Canteen on the table to heal your cuts. One of the chef's helpers comes flying out of the galley after you, but you're in a good position to take him out before he can fire a shot. You avoid most of the cleavers if you stay in a crouch and inch your way into the galley before putting several holes in the chef.

After your encounter with the chef, you discover more enemies in the galley. The number varies from two to four, depending on how many of them came out to meet you in the previous compartment. Pick up the two Medicinal Canteens on the wire racks to the left after you clear out the room.

Turn right around a wooden partition and move toward the next hallway. Two seamen start firing and a stray shot penetrates a steam pipe, preventing you from advancing. Crouch down and take out the seamen from long range. Turn off the steam by closing the large red valve on the right.

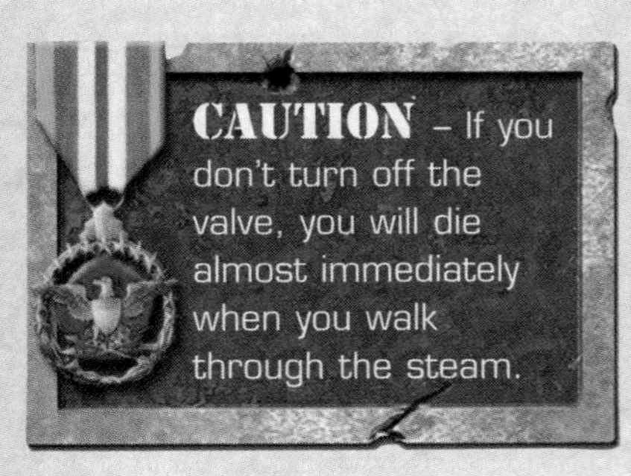

CAUTION – If you don't turn off the valve, you will die almost immediately when you walk through the steam.

Stay in your crouch and shimmy under the steam to the left side of the sub. Shoot the seaman in the corner and then turn off the second red valve at the end of the corridor. Turn around and walk to a small alcove on the left, where you find the third and final valve. With all of the steam valves closed, advance to the next door. Watch out for another enemy seaman to your left as you shut down the last valve.

Open the door to the engine room. You encounter four seamen armed with pistols. They don't respond immediately, so you have time to destroy them without suffering much health damage. At the end of the room, find a location to place a Demo Charge (move close to the flashing box and press the Action button to place the explosives). Back up or you could get hurt in the explosion. The explosion blows a hole in the bulkhead; crawl through and climb to another level. Before leaving, grab the Medicinal Canteens on the crate to your left.

SET EXPLOSIVES IN AFT TORPEDO ROOM

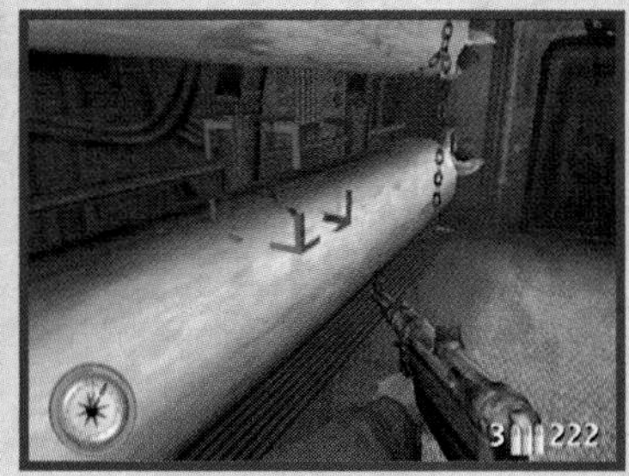

Crouch down and crawl through the pipes. Turn left at the first juncture and climb the ladder. You emerge behind a vent that leads into the torpedo room. Two seamen with machine guns guard the door at the end of the room in front of you. Start firing through the vent to eliminate them. Crawl into the compartment and place an Explosive Charge on the torpedo on the left side of the room. Pick up the 64-round ammo box just to the left of the door.

Make sure your machine gun has a fresh clip before opening the next hatch, because you must kill five seamen in the sleeping hold. Pick up two Medicinal Canteens on the berths.

DISABLE RADIO COMMUNICATIONS

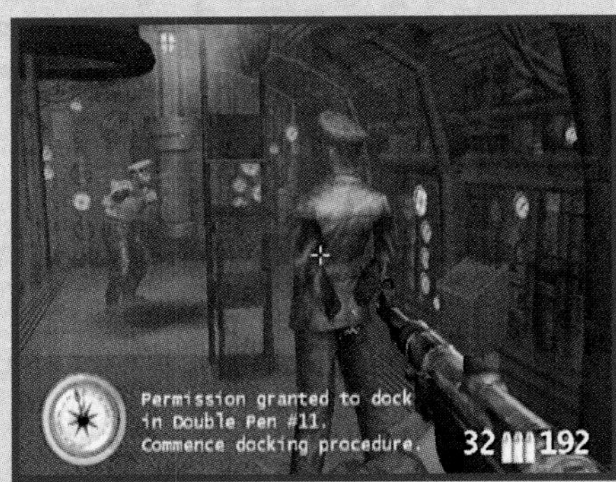

Open the next door and kill the Captain and his assistant. Pick up the ammo on the table to your left and continue to the next door, which leads to the radio room. Kill the communications officer and destroy the blue radio on the table. Watch out for another seaman armed with a submachine gun. Pick up a Medicinal Canteen on the table to your right.

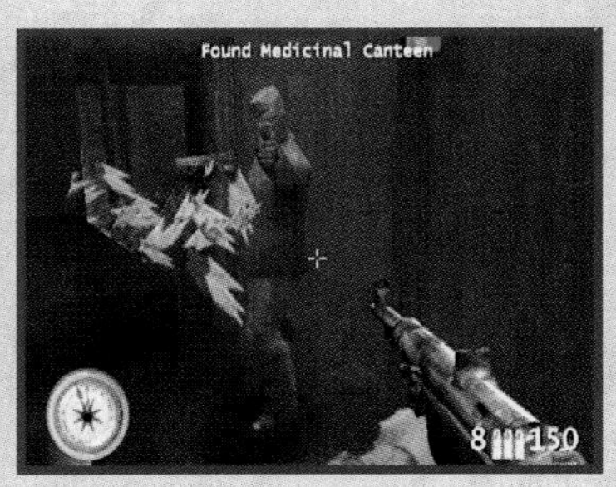

Edge around the corner until you have a shot at a German officer armed with a submachine gun. Collect the Medicinal Canteen and several ammo packs and then head to the next door. Another seaman pops out wielding a .45, but he is no match for your MP-40.

SET EXPLOSIVES IN FORE TORPEDO ROOM AND FIND ENIGMA CODE BOOK

Open the door into the fore torpedo room and take out the four seamen (armed with three pistols and one submachine gun). You face a tough group—make sure you have a full clip before entering the room. Set the final explosive charge and return to the officers' quarters. An officer armed with a submachine gun blocks your path. Dispatch him and then retrieve the Enigma Code Book located on the left side of the room in a cabinet (you must open the cabinet to retrieve the book). If you need it, grab the Field Surgeon Pack on top of the cabinet.

ESCAPE THROUGH EXIT HATCH

Continue down the hallway past the two radio rooms until you reach the main compartment. Climb the ladder to reach the exit hatch and complete your mission.

EYE OF THE STORM

MISSION OBJECTIVES

- Find Resistance Weapons Cache
- Find Rooftop Hatch near U-Boat Pen Two
- Destroy Supply Trucks
- Acquire Deployment Roster
- Infiltrate Wet Docks Facility

WEAPONS

- Colt .45
- MP-40
- Springfield Sniper Rifle
- Steil Grenades

FIND RESISTANCE WEAPONS CACHE

You are now on the dock, surrounded by unfriendly workers on the ground and deadly snipers above. Your first job: stay low behind the boxes, edge out to the corner, and take out the two workers, one near the light post and the other to the left of the crates (as you move to the edge of the boxes, you run right into a crate of Steil Grenades). From your hiding place, face the tower, east of your position, where a sniper has locked onto your position. A couple of accurate shots from your .45 will send him tumbling to his death. Run back behind the boxes near the civilians' former position and pick up the ammo.

Run to the shed in the southeast corner of the yard; you find bullets for your MP-40 and a Medicinal Canteen. Stay in a crouch and sneak back to the front of the shed to confront an approaching guard.

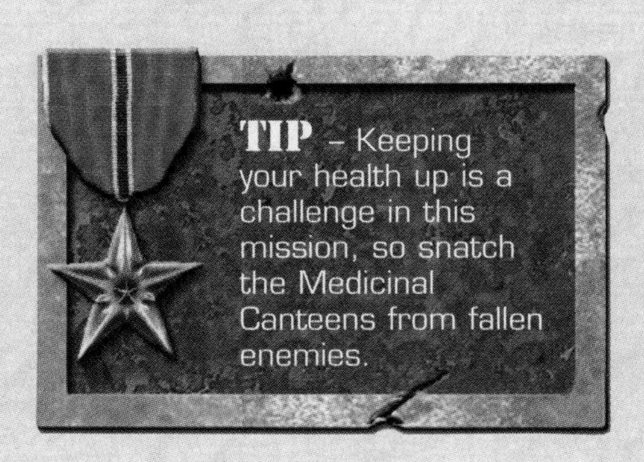

TIP – Keeping your health up is a challenge in this mission, so snatch the Medicinal Canteens from fallen enemies.

Run behind the truck parked near the warehouse and then hug the wall as you move to the stairs. Pick up the Steil Grenades in the alcove under the stairs, and climb up to the wall ladder on the third landing. Pull out your MP-40, scurry up the ladder to the roof, and get ready for a fight. The first soldier appears to your left, and he comes up firing. After taking him out, move straight to the north corner of the building and target the sniper crouching by the catwalk that connects the two buildings.

Your first objective lies just across the catwalk. Race across and turn right to collect the Resistance Weapons Cache. Open the suitcase to retrieve the Springfield Sniper Rifle and Demolition Charges.

FIND ROOFTOP HATCH NEAR U-BOAT PEN TWO

Armed with the Springfield, take on the snipers scattered around and above you. From your position near the suitcase, turn south toward the water tower where two snipers patrol on the roof. Two quick head shots, and you move on.

Walk back to the other roof, where you contend with four snipers. Turn right when you exit the catwalk and hug the wall of the building as you move to the right. When you reach the northwest corner, pop up and plug the sniper in worker clothes, positioned directly in front of the crane. Only his head sticks out above the wall, so you need an accurate shot here.

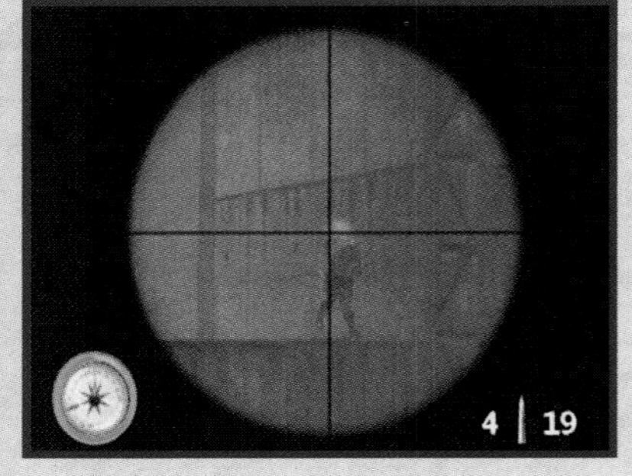

Continue to your left around the building. At the next corner, look to your left (southeast) to target a sniper standing on a flat roof in front of the brick building.

At the next corner, turn to the north, and fix your scope on the water tower where another sniper awaits you. The sniper cannot see you from your position, so take your time and take him out.

One more to go. Stay in a crouch and use the wall for cover as you finish your walk around the building, ending up in the southwest corner. Keep your head down and move to the northeast corner of the roof. As you approach the wall, you draw fire from a sailor positioned on the deck of a destroyer, near the gun turret. Pop up and wax him to eliminate the fourth and final sniper.

With the snipers cleared, you can now watch your handiwork. Run back to the roof ladder and watch the submarine explode. Shortly after the explosion, four German soldiers rush onto the dock, southwest of your position at the ladder. Jump down to the next landing and use your Springfield to target the first three soldiers who come into view. The last soldier hides behind the large cluster of boxes, so advance along the railing on the left for a better shot. After you nail all four, pick up the Medicinal Canteen and Field Surgeon Pack near the stack of crates on the left side of the dock.

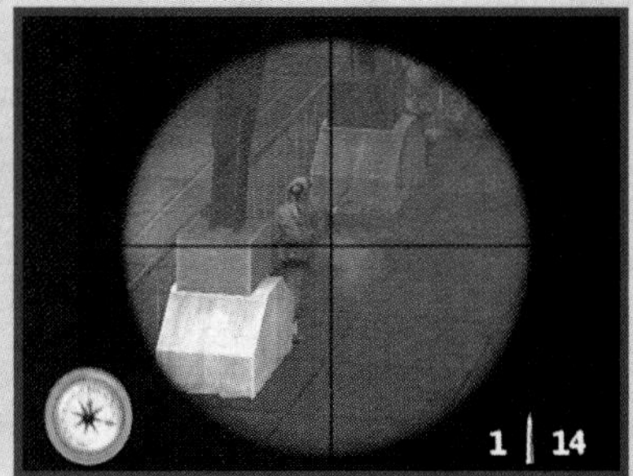

You have two more sailors to contend with on the destroyer deck. The first one snipes at you with his rifle before racing to man the fixed machine gun. If you miss him as he sprints across the ship, train your scope on the machine gun mounted on a railing near the bow. When he grabs hold, hit him. With your Springfield loaded, keep your scope on the gun and wait for the second sailor to make a run for the machine gun. You might take one or two rifle hits before he makes his move, but this is a welcome alternative to being raked by the heavy machine gun.

Work your way around the building. A guard appears near the end of the building. Use your Springfield to take him out. Reload and go to the corner of the building. Nail the two sailors firing at you from the vicinity of the Kubelwagen and then look for a civilian walking from right to left. Continue along the passageway, picking up ammo discards as you go. Pull out your MP-40, move to the corner of the building on the left, and wait for a dock worker to show up. Take him out, turn the corner, and kill his partner.

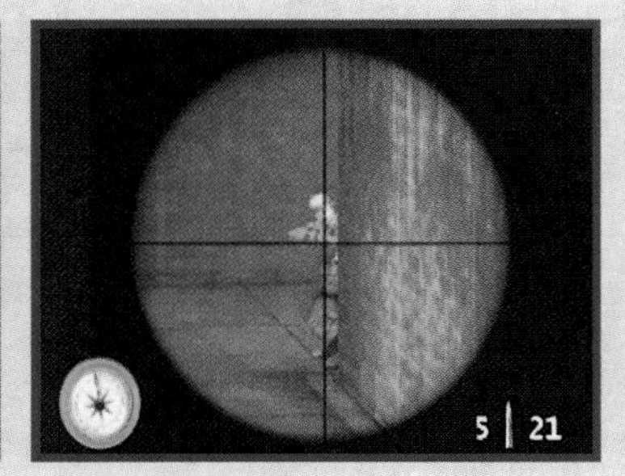

As you approach the end of the passageway, you receive fire from a guard at the top of the stairs. Dispatch him and then use your Springfield to hit the soldier at the far northern end of the passageway. Make a detour to the left into an alcove containing several wooden boxes. Three of the boxes contain health pickups. Blast them to reveal two Medicinal Canteens and a Medical Kit.

Top off your health—you need it for the next segment. Grab your MP-40, walk down the stairs, and look around the corner. Retreat and shoot the two soldiers who give chase. Pop out again and nail another guard foolish enough to have his back turned to you. If you wait a little longer, a fourth soldier will come after you. Reduce the enemy forces closest to you *before* you advance around the corner, because you must contend with fog and heavy fire coming from a distance.

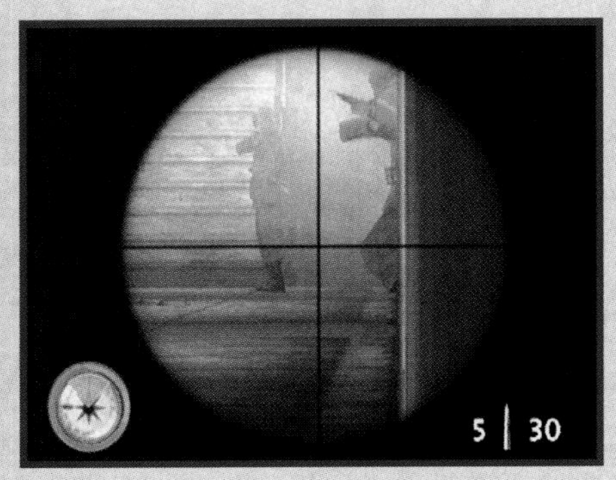

Visibility is poor here, so crouch down and edge around the corner until you spot a rifle sticking out from an alcove on the right. Keep inching forward until the German soldier pops out. Shoot him and then collect the ammo left behind (on the ground, and in the alcove). Move forward to the next alcove; take the MP-40 bullets and Medicinal Canteen.

With your Springfield fully loaded, advance towards the stairs, keeping a close eye on the right upper railing where a sniper lurks. Take him out and proceed up the stairs. Two more German soldiers wait above, but the fog has cleared so they're easy pickings. Swing your Springfield up and to the left to target the sniper on the water tower.

Pick up the Medicinal Canteens and move along the wall on the left until you see a sniper walking on top of a train car. Shoot him and then swing your rifle to the left to hit a guard up on the catwalk. Move up a few more paces and sweep your scope to the right of the boxcar where you see an armed civilian. The next shot is more challenging. At the base of the steel tower on the other side of the yard, an armed civilian lurks behind the girders. Take your time and bag him. Eliminating these enemies now will make your upcoming maneuvers in the train yard that much easier.

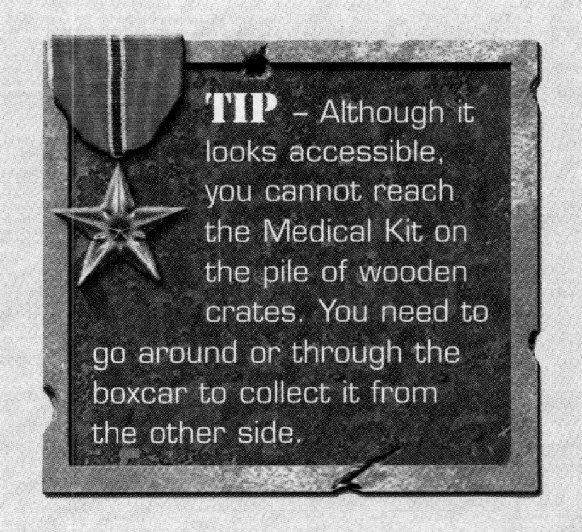

Move to the opposite wall, crouch, and inch your way around the corner, keeping your rifle trained to the right. When you see sandbags behind the fuel drum, an MG-42 gunner is not far behind. Inch out a little more to see him standing to the right of the gun. He sees you and jumps behind the MG-42, but you nail him before he squeezes the trigger. With the machine-gun nest vacated, dart out and to the left to retrieve the Springfield and MP-40 ammo in the alley.

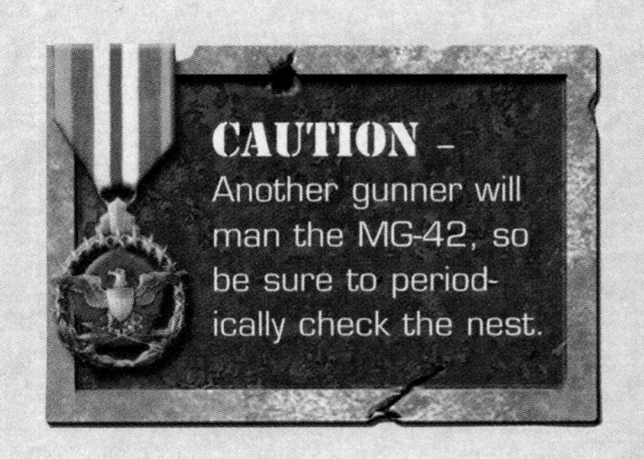

You must get around the boxcar to the ladder that takes you into the north warehouse. But first, look out for the sniper on the warehouse roof behind you. Run into the alleyway ahead and to the right, and pick up the ammo. Before you ice the sniper, take out the two German guards with your Springfield, reload, and inch to the corner with your gun raised. You have a good shot at the rooftop sniper.

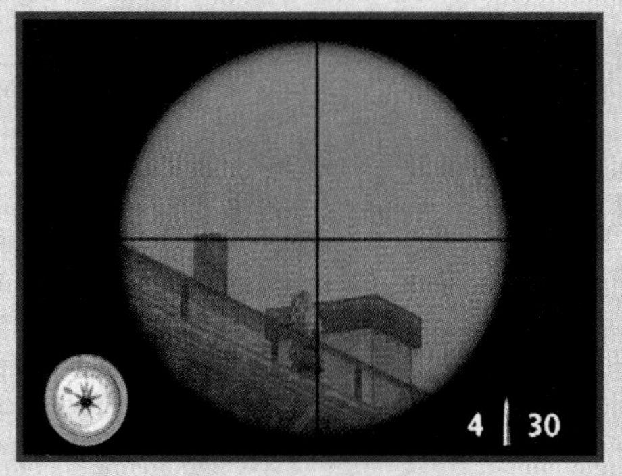

Now you can run for the train. Grab your MP-40 and dash across the street, hugging the right side of the train cars. As you approach the stairway, two civilians come charging into view on the right. Take them out and hop onto the boxcar to collect the Field Surgeon Pack. Jump out on the other side. To snag the Field Surgeon Pack on the stack of crates, run back in the direction from which you came. A civilian pops out of the doorway on the right as you run to the crates, so stay alert.

With your health fully charged you can climb the roof ladder ahead and to your right. However, if your health is low, there's a Medical Kit (and ammo) on a flatbed car behind the last boxcar. As you reach the top of the ladder, the Germans announce your presence on the rooftop. Take cover behind the chimney and look to the east, where two soldiers pepper you from the next chimney. Eliminate them and then use your Springfield to kill another soldier on the far side of the roof. Run to the next chimney, collect the two Medicinal Canteens left behind and then continue to the third chimney, where you confront another guard. Bear to the right after the last chimney and continue along the ramp to the roof hatch.

DESTROY SUPPLY TRUCKS

Grab a Steil Grenade and climb down through the hatch onto the walkway below. It seems like the entire German army has a bead on you from the warehouse floor, but you find just a ragtag group of workers and sailors. But they still use real bullets, so use the pillar for cover and start lobbing Grenades. Keep tossing Grenades until you clear out several of the shooters and then drop down onto the floor of the warehouse to finish off the stragglers.

Train your MP-40 on the door at the north side of the warehouse where several sailors appear. After you eliminate them, run to the other ladder (not the one you came down on). Climb up to the ledge to gather a Medical Kit and assorted ammo. You'll need it!

Return once more to the floor (you can jump down without suffering damage), work your way to the north, and exit through the door. Depending on your success on the catwalk, a few sailors may still block your path. Move past the first stack of supplies and take cover at the next one, so you can effectively handle the German soldiers as they arrive on the scene. Move north until you reach the roadway. Edge around the corner of the building on the right and look to the east, where a sniper perches in a tower. Use your Springfield to send him to the ground floor.

TIP – If you take several hits in the initial confrontation with the workers, go back to the alley you just passed. Take a left, and then another left, and look for the Field Surgeon Pack behind the ventilation unit. Keep your MP-40 handy, because you will encounter a few soldiers and workers along the way.

Move east along the roadway. The large stacking of crates on the right signals the beginning of the truck yard. Several armed workers race up as you approach the gates, so make sure you have a full clip in your MP-40. After you clear the yard, leave Demo Charges at the front of the three supply trucks, working your way from right to left. There is a very short delay before each charge explodes—don't linger near the trucks once you set them. After the last charge, run to the corner of the yard and take cover behind the shed.

The explosions set off the alarm, which brings another wave of angry truckers. Use your Springfield to sweep the shipping dock until you nail them all (in both the yard and dock) before you venture out. The end of this mission approaches, and losing your life now would inconvenience you, to say the least.

ACQUIRE DEPLOYMENT ROSTER

Walk up the ramp into the warehouse, where armed workers fire on you. Kill them and move into the hallway where more guards aim at you. Clear the hall and go back to the loading area to turn off the alarm. Return to the hallway and enter the office to find the Deployment Roster.

As you leave the office, another armed worker appears. Take care of him and return to the loading dock, where more guards await. Shoot them from the doorway and move cautiously out on the dock. More armed workers and guards appear—watch your back! Another armed worker will pop out of the hallway behind you.

INFILTRATE WET DOCKS FACILITY

Clean out the dock, walk out and to your left, and you see another supply truck parked beneath an overhead walkway. Set your last Demo Charge and step back. The exploding truck brings down the walkway, providing you a route to the wet docks facility. Hop onto the crates to the catwalk. Cross to the next building, collect the ammo to your left, and follow the path to the wet docks facility below. Congratulations, you just completed Eye of the Storm!

A CHANCE MEETING

MISSION OBJECTIVES

- Sabotage Engines in Research Facility
- Acquire Engine Blueprints
- Infiltrate U-Boat Bunker
- Destroy All U-Boats
- Blow Up Fuel Depot
- Find Dock Gates

WEAPONS

- Colt .45
- MP-40
- Springfield Sniper Rifle
- Steil Grenades

SABOTAGE ENGINES IN RESEARCH FACILITY

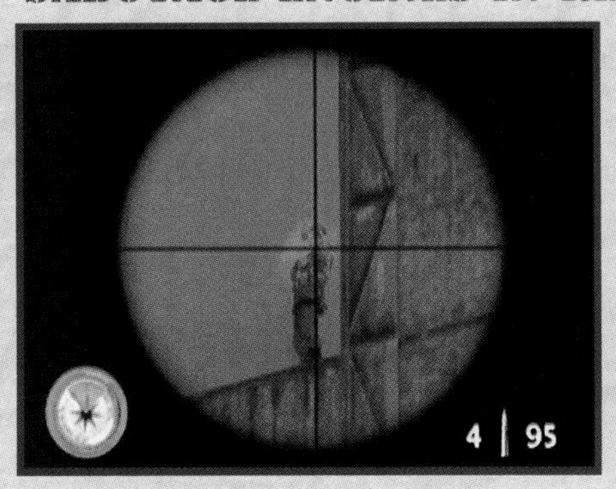

As the mission begins, you stand on a stack of crates overlooking the facility. Before jumping down, use your Springfield to shoot the sniper on the lower section of the brick building to the northeast. Switch to your MP-40 and drop down off the crates. Dispatch the soldiers on either side, and go to the left, picking up discarded ammo and Medicinal Canteens. Check around the corner for Grenades.

Secure the area and proceed north to a narrow alleyway that leads to the train tracks. Expect heavy fire from German soldiers on either side of the alley and behind the stacked boxes on the flatcar. As you emerge from the alley, watch out for the sniper atop the boxcar on the left.

Eliminate the soldiers around the flatcar, and run to the right, where you find several Medicinal Canteens. Move to the other side of the train and work your way back; pick up the ammo and Field Surgeon Pack in the first boxcar.

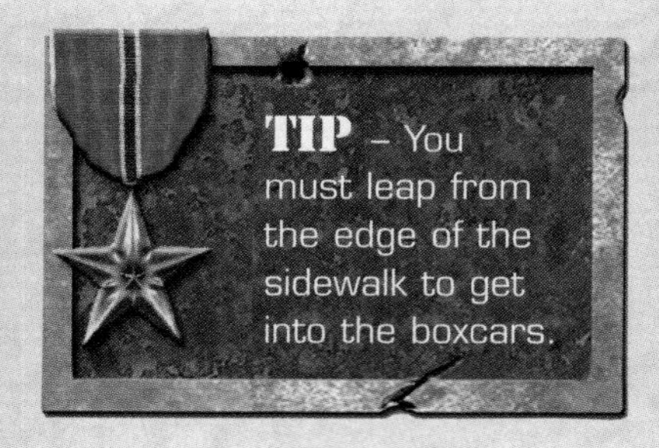

TIP – You must leap from the edge of the sidewalk to get into the boxcars.

At the last boxcar, flip the switch to release the open flatcar (with the MG-42), causing it to roll to the end of the track. Cross to the other side of the tracks, crouch down, and move behind the wooden boxes. Jump onto the boxes, man the MG-42, and lay waste to the yard. Keep firing until you blow up the fuel barrels and take out all of the German soldiers who respond. Remember the sniper in the tower on the left side of the yard and the machine gunner positioned behind the sandbags at the base of the tower.

The MG-42 did its job, but expect plenty of resistance ahead. Enter the yard and train your Springfield on a machine gunner firing from the pickup truck on the right. Pick him off before he makes you his next prize. When his gun falls silent, hop onto his truck and pick up the Field Surgeon Pack, MP-40 bullets, and Grenades. Train the Springfield on another truck north of your position where another soldier lies in wait. Look halfway up the tower and take out the sniper firing from the platform to the left.

Cross the road and check out the warehouse for ammo. From the warehouse, train your Springfield on the MG-42 nest in front of the tower (north of your position). When they see you, three sailors will take turns manning the gun, so exercise patience and shoot them all.

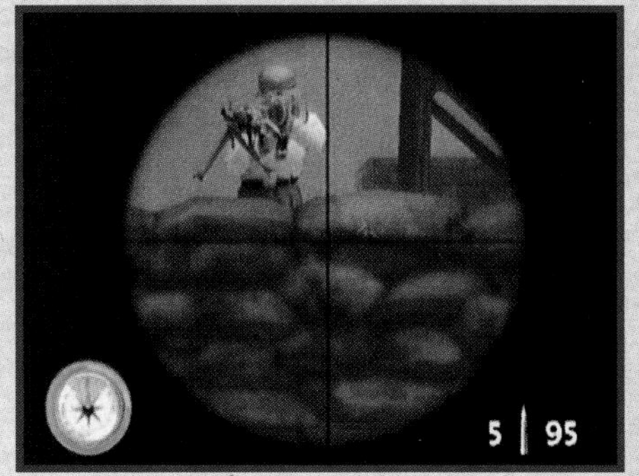

Proceed toward the MG-42 and turn left, wrapping around the building. Watch for the soldier who pops out from behind the large ventilation unit. At the corner, take out two elevated snipers before you continue to your left, around the building. Walk past the Kubelwagen and cross to the other side. Pick up the MP-40 bullets around the corner. From here, you can explore the area to the left for ammo and medical supplies.

If you have all the supplies you need, inch around the corner of the building, and drop off the ledge. Here you will find the engines and blueprints, so look sharp. Pick off one or both of the guards with your Springfield. Another worker will drop down off the dock, so switch weapons quickly and wax him. Continue into the building and down the hallway, which leads to the engine facility.

Open the door, back up, and kill the scientist with your Springfield; switch to your MP-40 to eliminate the other workers who rush toward the door. A Field Surgeon Pack is on the table to the right, but you must first take care of the workers down below and to the left.

Time to blow up all three engines; remember to stay clear after setting the Demo Charges! When the third engine blows, German soldiers rush into the room from the north, so prepare to return fire. After this first wave, destroy the wooden boxes in the south corner of the room for more ammo and a Field Surgeon Pack. Exit the room to the northwest.

ACQUIRE ENGINE BLUEPRINTS

Dispatch the guard in the hallway and continue to the next corner on the left. With your Springfield, target the worker or the fuel barrel at the other end of the room. Continue around the corner, which takes you to a torpedo room. Kill the two armed workers, and blow up the boxes in the far corner of the room to reveal more ammo.

The next area of the warehouse contains the blueprints. Edge around the corner and eliminate the two white coats. Grab the Medical Kit and the blueprints, then turn around to shoot another worker as he comes into the room.

INFILTRATE U-BOAT BUNKER

Enter the door to the north, and turn left. Follow the hallway until you reach another large warehouse area. Back up into the corner and wait until you see the scientist. Pop him with the Springfield, inch forward, and then swing your rifle up to shoot the worker on top of the submarine hull. A second worker attacks from a scaffolding as you move into view. Another armed worker appears from the north door, your eventual destination. Take care of him, check the rest of the room, and pick up the Medical Kit on the table in the northwest corner.

Go up the stairs and turn left. Use your MP-40 to blow out the wall grate and enter the tunnel. After picking up the Medicinal Canteen, you get your first look at Herr Stermgeist, who is not amused by your sabotage. Shoot your way around the catwalk and enter the door in the northeast corner. Grab the Medicinal Canteen in the first alcove on your left and continue to the intersection. The next left-hand turn takes you to the control room; it is well guarded, so check your MP-40 clip.

DESTROY ALL U-BOATS

Eliminate the two white coats and the officer, and turn off the wall alarm. Move to the control panel and press the Action button to activate the switch. The overhead track drops a torpedo on the U-boat below. Three more to go. The explosion sends armed sailors scurrying to your location, so don't linger here.

Leave the control room, walk down the hallway and turn left, which brings you to the stairs. Descend, and prepare for heavy fire from ahead and to your right. Fight your way around the catwalk to the stern of the boat, and go up the stairs on the far side.

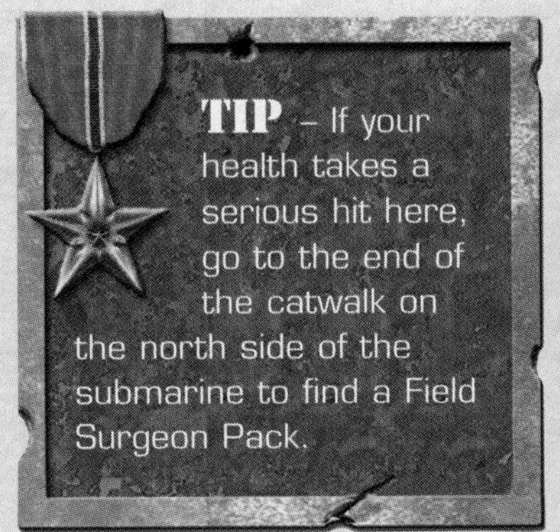

TIP – If your health takes a serious hit here, go to the end of the catwalk on the north side of the submarine to find a Field Surgeon Pack.

Follow the hallway around to another set of stairs, eliminating another guard along the way. Climb the stairs and get ready for your toughest fight yet. If you have a good supply of Grenades, toss a few over the side to even the odds a little. Then inch up with your Springfield and take out the German soldiers firing from the deck of the U-boat. Race out onto the catwalk and run as far as possible to the right. From here, pick off the remaining soldiers.

BLOW UP FUEL DEPOT

After you clear the room, climb down the ladder to the deck below. Walk to the catwalk leading to the U-boat and climb on board. Take over the deck gun and get ready to blast the German soldiers who come streaming through the left-hand door. When the center door opens, lob a few shells at the fuel depot to turn it into a big bonfire. Make sure you blow up the stack of crates to the northeast when manning the gun (to the right of the bay doors) in order to reach the bridge.

FIND DOCK GATES

Now you can access the aft deck of the U-boat. Climb down off the deck gun, exit the facility through the left-hand door and come back through the center door. Walk through the chain-link door and onto the aft catwalk. Place your last Demo Charge and race outside to watch the explosion. All of the U-boats go up in flames! Make your way to the dock gates to finish the mission.

A NEEDLE IN A HAYSTACK

ROUGH LANDING

MISSION OBJECTIVES

- Protect Corporal Barnes as He Destroys Tanks
- Find Kerosene
- Protect Corporal Barnes as He Destroys Tanks (Continued)
- Create Distraction to Open City Gates

WEAPONS

- Colt .45
- M1 Garand
- Thompson SMG

PROTECT CORPORAL BARNES AS HE DESTROYS TANKS

After the paratroop drop, you meet with Barnes, who heads down the road after a brief introduction. A fellow paratrooper has his chute caught on a windmill blade. He implores you to help him, but a Nazi bullet seals his fate. Approach the house on the left and shoot the German officer who is terrorizing a civilian.

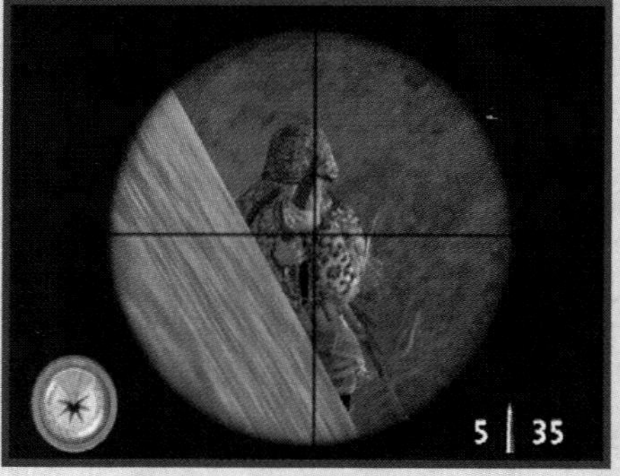

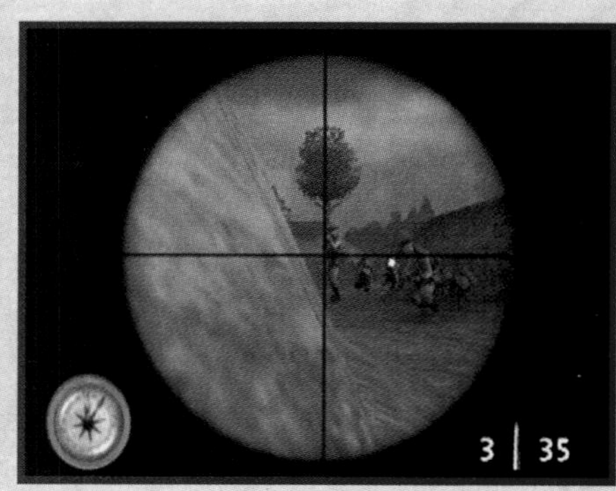

As you approach the house, you receive fire from down the road. Also, if you don't quickly kill the German officer in the house, he will start shooting. Pause to the right of the car and use your sniper rifle to take out the three German soldiers lying in ambush around the bend in the road. As you advance, several German soldiers move in and start firing. Switch to your Thompson because the Springfield takes too long to aim, shoot, and reload. Barnes will help, but fire quickly to keep him from taking too much punishment. Remember, he must survive long enough to take out the five tanks.

Another trio of German soldiers waits around the next bend, so proceed with caution. As the road turns toward the windmill, you encounter enemy soldiers near the haystacks, in front of the fence, and down the road by the rock wall. Take them out from long range and continue down the road.

The first tank is ahead and to the right, guarded by three soldiers (actually two, because one of them runs away when you start firing). After you kill the two guards, Barnes places his charge at the back of the truck. For a quick kill, shoot the red gas can when the German soldiers are near it. In addition to dispatching the guards, avoid the tank's main gun, which can kill you with just a couple of hits. Watch the turret. When it starts swinging towards you, get out of sight (don't just duck behind the tree). After the tank blows, look for the third German soldier as he shoots at you from a distance. Keep track of him or he could put an early end to the mission. Check out the lean-to for a Medicinal Canteen and Thompson rounds.

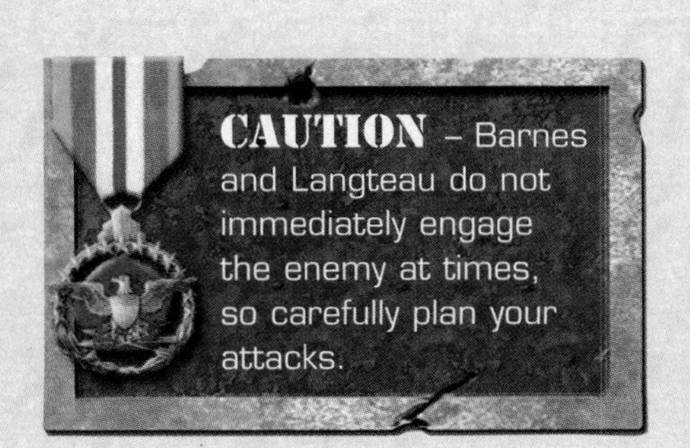

CAUTION – Barnes and Langteau do not immediately engage the enemy at times, so carefully plan your attacks.

While the first tank smolders, continue down the road and across the bridge, where you meet with another Airborne soldier, Langteau. He's waiting under a lean-to on the left, so don't shoot him. Pick up 20 rounds of Thompson ammo and five Grenades. Continue north and your two buddies follow you.

Resume your course around the winding road, which brings you to a bridge guarded by a lone German soldier. You can take him out quickly, but he's not alone. As you advance toward the bridge, another German soldier starts firing, and by the time you are mid-span, several more join in from the right. Switch to the Thompson and engage the enemy on both sides of the road. Work quickly, because Barnes and Langteau receive heavy fire as they run ahead into the village. You know they've secured the village when Barnes announces his intent to go for the second tank.

FIND KEROSENE

The path winds through the hills and reaches a large clearing where a German officer harasses a farmer. Take the officer out, along with his two buddies, and continue to the northeast toward a covered bridge. Langteau and Barnes scurry ahead, so don't delay, because more Germans await you all on the other side.

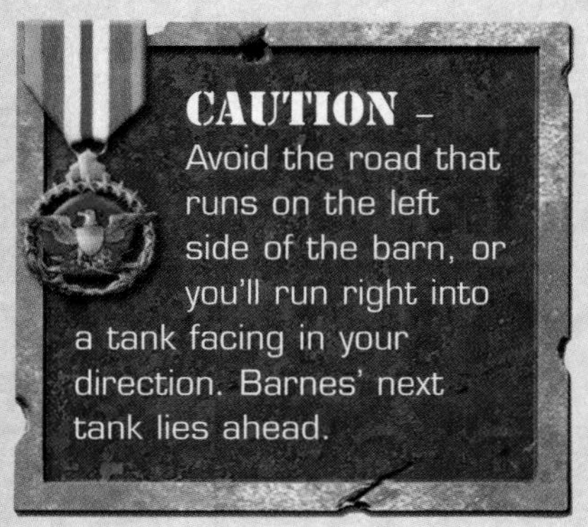

CAUTION – Avoid the road that runs on the left side of the barn, or you'll run right into a tank facing in your direction. Barnes' next tank lies ahead.

As you approach the bridge, note the thick black smoke rising on the other side. Move slowly across the bridge and you hear the sound of a crackling fire. Four German soldiers take a break from the action, but they respond to your movement and rush the bridge. Fortunately, you can stay hidden on the left side and pick them off as they run to the bridge. Walk to the left side of the fire and pick up the Kerosene.

PROTECT CORPORAL BARNES AS HE DESTROYS TANKS (CONTINUED)

The path leads into a clearing, and a lone sniper starts firing. He proves elusive, especially when he starts rolling around on the ground, but you can take him out with your Springfield. Stay on the left side of the path and edge very slowly toward the field until you see a wooden box and a gas can to the left. Do not move out any further or the tank will pulverize you. Shoot the gas can to cause an explosion that kills a second German soldier. Now the tank knows your location and you receive a hit. Stay back and look for a third sniper in the field. Destroy him and race onto the field and bear to the right as Barnes rushes the tank. This action unfolds very quickly, so eliminate all three soldiers *before* Barnes runs to the tank, or they'll cut him down. After the third tank explodes, scour the area for health pickups: you probably need them.

TIP – Ammo and health pickups are rare in this mission, so remember to scoop up ammo from dead Germans, or you may run out of bullets before the end of the mission.

Leave the clearing and continue along the path, where you encounter a group of three Germans. Use your Thompson or lob a Grenade to take them out: they are too close for your rifle. Load your Springfield as you approach the next clearing, where you eliminate no fewer than six deadly snipers. Stay within the protection of the path until all six German soldiers are dead!

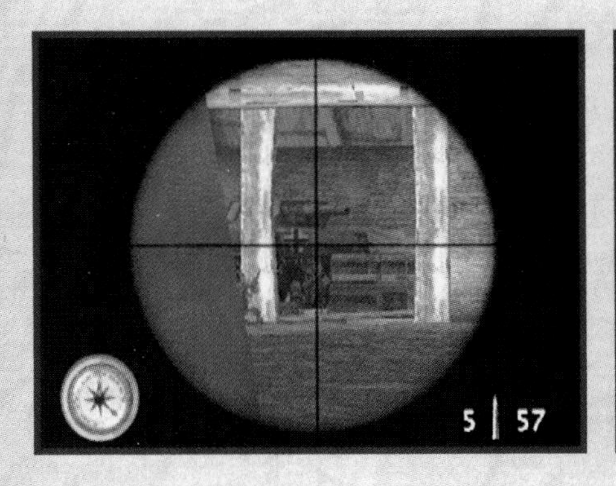

Now for the tank. Edge out on the left, just far enough to target a German sniper sprawled in front of the tank hidden inside a building. It's almost impossible to hit the sniper, so aim for the fuel can instead. After you ice the sniper, run out past the building to provide cover for Barnes as he advances to the fourth tank. After the explosion, pick up the ammo and Medical Kit in the garage. Look for another Medicinal Canteen on the hill to the right.

Continue along the path and pick up the ammo near the haystacks on the left. As the path turns toward the north, you see a windmill. If you get there first, you'll run into a sniper on the ledge. However, if you hang back to forage, Barnes and Langteau will probably take care of him and two other German soldiers. Continue along the path until you see the edge of a brown house on the left side of the road. Stop, and target the first two German soldiers from a distance.

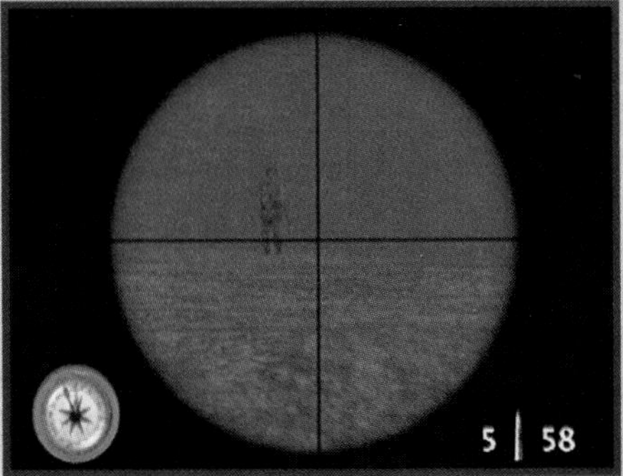

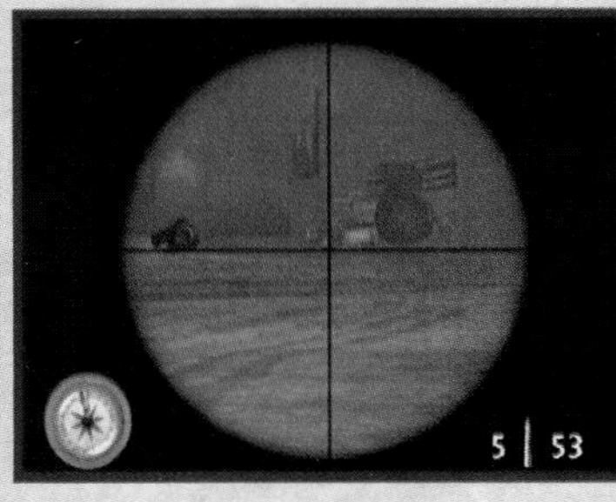

The fighting gets heavy in a hurry, as six more German soldiers join the fray. You have stumbled on a Nebelwurfer (rocket launcher) site, and the Germans do not want to give it up. Target the gas cans near the Nebelwurfer to take out multiple enemies. Keep firing and stay close to Barnes and Langteau as they advance. They've landed in the thick of things, and you don't want to lose them now. As you move closer, you see the tank off to the right, but this time Barnes does not set a charge. You must man the Nebelwurfer and press the Action button to launch a salvo at the tank. One more to go.

Follow the winding path until you come to a large clearing: a mortar field. Wait for Barnes to make the first move and then follow him around the perimeter of the field to avoid the mortar fire. Return fire as you move, but stay behind Barnes or you risk getting blown up. The last tank is up ahead—with German soldiers around it.

Keep following Barnes around the buildings, pausing only to pick up a Medical Kit and assorted ammo. Continue to the right of the haystacks and you see the last tank, along with more German soldiers. Unfortunately, the tank commander also sees you.

When the tank starts firing, run back around the left side of the house and target the fuel can and drum near the rear of the tank. The explosion should take care of the remaining soldiers. The mortar fire continues as Barnes moves in to blow up the fifth and final tank. As the tank smolders, pick up two Medicinal Canteens and some ammo.

CREATE DISTRACTION TO OPEN CITY GATES

Continue along the path, dispatching one more German soldier along the way. When you reach the intersection, Barnes bids you farewell, and you continue north towards the windmill and your final objective.

Follow the path toward the windmill. There's a haystack to the right and a large brick building with a closed gate to the left. Approach the haystack and press the Action button to ignite it. This causes the outer doors of the building to swing open and four German soldiers charge out firing. Kill them and walk toward the inner gates to complete the mission.

THE GOLDEN LION

MISSION OBJECTIVES

- Locate Tools to Sabotage Vehicles
- Sabotage Motor Pool to Prevent Pursuit
- Meet Operative at Garage
- Get an Officer's Uniform
- Meet Contact in Golden Lion Bar

WEAPONS

- Silenced Pistol
- Springfield Sniper Rifle
- Thompson SMG
- Mark II Grenades

LOCATE TOOLS TO SABOTAGE VEHICLES

Grab a Grenade and edge up along the brick wall on your right until you see two German soldiers near an MG-42. Toss the Grenade, wait for it to blow up, and then leap behind the machine gun. Swing it over to the right and wait for several German soldiers to wander into your line of fire. After killing them, swing the gun to the left to target two more soldiers. When all falls quiet, race into the street to collect the ammo and Medicinal Canteen, but watch out for stragglers lurking around the house on either side.

When the shooting stops, follow the wall to the right, and turn right onto the next street to collect a Medical Kit and ammo. Exit this area to the right and edge along the right-hand wall until you reach the corner. Two soldiers wait in the courtyard to your right. You can target the first one from afar with your Springfield, or toss a Grenade over the wall. Then grab your Thompson, crouch down, and approach the opening until you draw out the second soldier. Enter the courtyard and pick up the ammo and Medicinal Canteen.

Move north toward the canal with your Springfield loaded and ready. Bear to the left, behind the garbage cans, and look for the lone sentry on the other side. Take him out, cross over to the other side, and look across the canal to your left, where you find a pair of soldiers. Run to the left side and inch forward, looking across the canal to your right—there are two more soldiers, both stationary (one is well hidden behind a fence).

CAUTION – If you cannot quickly shoot the second pair, they will eventually rush your position. Switch to the Thompson and gun them down before they get too close. Then go back to the Springfield and continue tracking the other two soldiers across the canal.

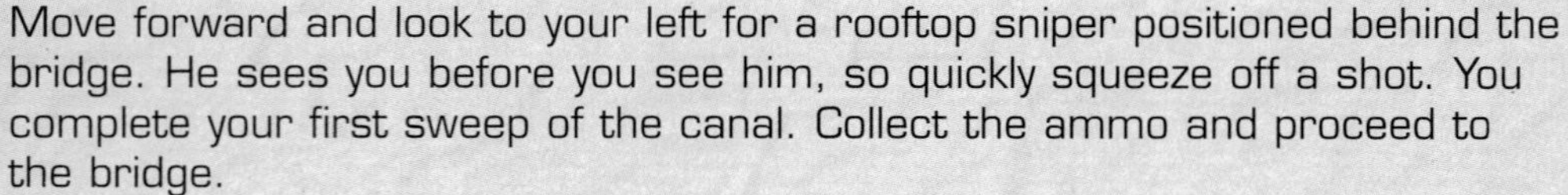

Move forward and look to your left for a rooftop sniper positioned behind the bridge. He sees you before you see him, so quickly squeeze off a shot. You complete your first sweep of the canal. Collect the ammo and proceed to the bridge.

Cross the bridge and turn to your right, walking to the barrier where you find some Grenades and a Medicinal Canteen. Avoid blasting the crates and barrels—there's nothing inside. Turn around and walk almost to the other end of the sidewalk, turning right into a narrow courtyard at the Meubel's sign. As you advance through the courtyard to the north, note the alarm on the left-hand wall up ahead. When the shooting starts, disable this alarm to secure the courtyard and prevent the Germans from overrunning your position.

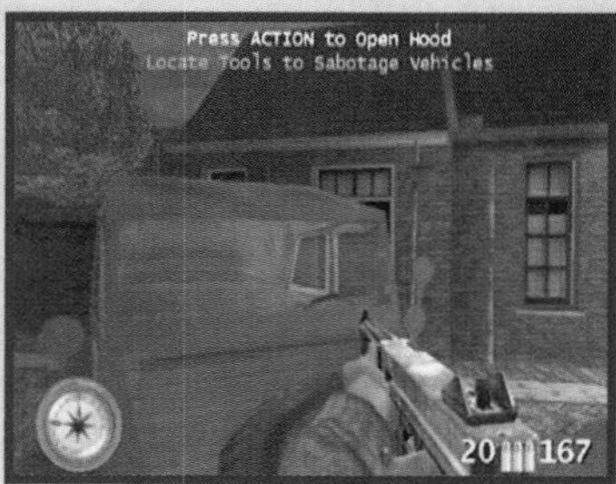

Grab a Grenade and ease your way into the courtyard. When you see the truck, lob several Grenades from right to left, with the last one in the vicinity of the alarm. You may need to take out the survivor with your Springfield. After you deal with everyone, collect the ammo in the courtyard and open the hood of the Kubelwagen to access a Medical Kit.

Your next destination lies on the other side of the west gate (green double doors), but first check your original point of entry to the south. If you left anyone alive on the canal, he might appear as a sniper on the bridge. Proceed through the green doors and turn right to enter one of the few courtyards in this mission that aren't crawling with enemy soldiers. Open the toolbox on the table to retrieve the necessary tools for sabotaging vehicles. Walk to the trunk of the Kubelwagen (that's where you'll find its engine), and press the Action button to snip the wires. Finally, open the car's hood to reveal Silenced Pistol bullets and a Medical Kit.

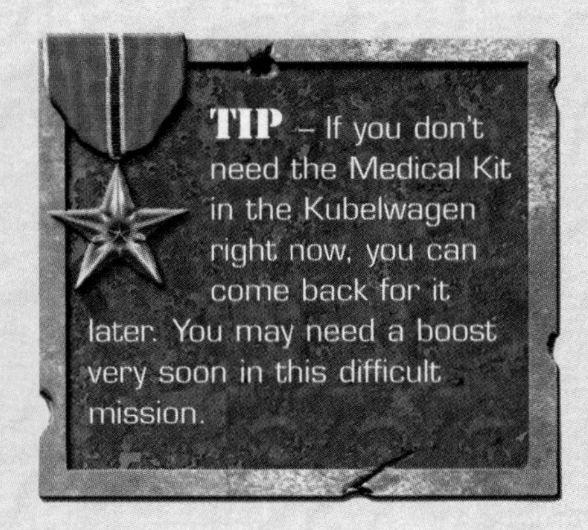

TIP – If you don't need the Medical Kit in the Kubelwagen right now, you can come back for it later. You may need a boost very soon in this difficult mission.

SABOTAGE MOTOR POOL TO PREVENT PURSUIT

Continue your mission in the adjacent courtyard where you sabotage three more vehicles. After you finish the last vehicle, you receive a message that the Resistance has been signaled. Now you must rendezvous with the operative.

MEET OPERATIVE AT GARAGE

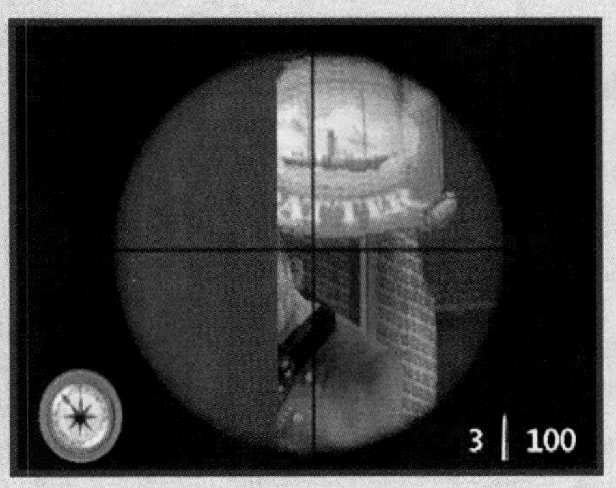

Go back to the canal, where you travel eastbound to meet the operative. However, this isn't a stroll in the park. As you exit Meubel's to the left, watch for a guard walking in your direction. The actual number of soldiers you encounter along the way depends on how many you neutralized earlier. As you curve around and catch your first glimpse of the barbed-wire barrier, watch for a rifle sticking out on the left. Inch your way forward until you can shoot your enemy with your Springfield. When you reach the intersection, turn left and look for a small door on the right.

Follow the path until it empties into a small yard. Open the door to meet the operative, Fox. He wants you to clear the area of Germans and sabotage the cars before he drives out in his truck. Pick up the ammo and Field Surgeon Pack on the other side of the truck before you venture out of the garage. Take the Grenades under the table.

The enemy makes you look for them. Your first clear shot, a sentry, is at the top of the stairs across the street. Try to shoot him with the Springfield, but don't kick yourself if you miss what looks like a perfect head shot. The sentry drops out of sight and two other soldiers come running to the garage. Switch to your Thompson, crouch down to the right of the car, and shoot them when they arrive.

Stay within the safety of the garage until you even the odds a little. If you run out and back, the sniper on the stairs will pop his head up just long enough for you to blow it off. With the sniper out of the way, hug the buildings on the right and run across the courtyard to the alcove. Edge out with your Springfield and take out the soldier on the other side of the courtyard, right over the hood of the black car. After the shot, switch to the Thompson, back up a little, and get ready for another soldier who charges your position.

When the alarm goes off, all hell breaks loose. Back up and sweep your Springfield up to take out the rooftop sniper positioned above and to the right of the garage. When he goes down, look to the right for another sniper up high.

After another soldier rushes toward you, grab your Springfield and sneak up the stairs, staying in a crouch. That infernal alarm lies west of your position; you can take it out if you edge out far enough. By disabling the alarm you've secured the area, but don't start feeling too safe just yet.

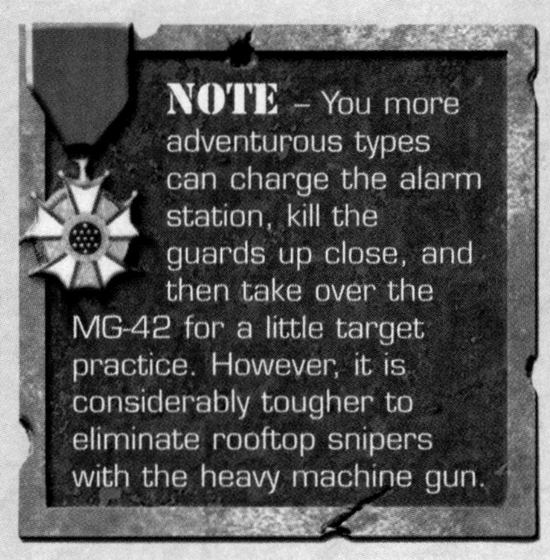

NOTE – You more adventurous types can charge the alarm station, kill the guards up close, and then take over the MG-42 for a little target practice. However, it is considerably tougher to eliminate rooftop snipers with the heavy machine gun.

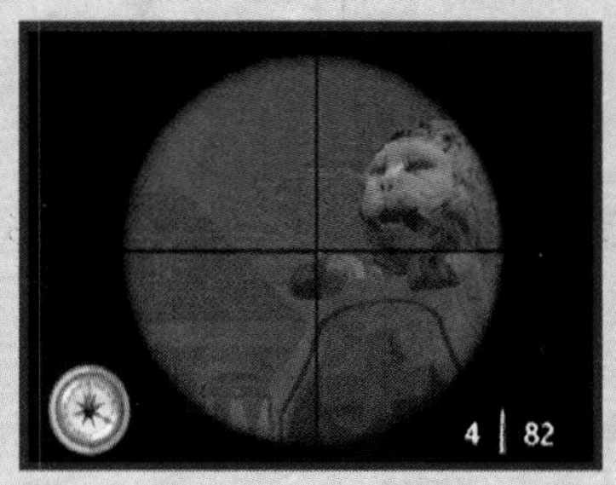

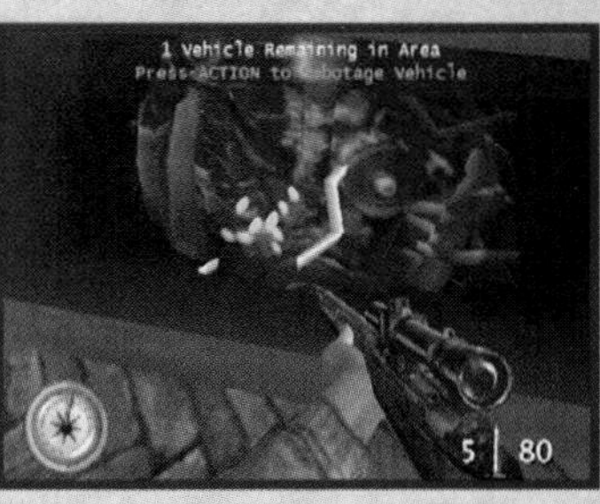

Go down the stairs and look for a sniper directly above the statue of a lion (look over the lion's left paw). Even though you haven't completely cleaned out the yard, you can still begin breaking cars. Sneak up to the black car and press the Action button when you get in front of the hood. Wreck the Kubelwagen next. One more car remains: another Kubelwagen on the west side of the courtyard.

If you need a health boost, run back to the garage and grab the Field Surgeon Pack next to the passenger side of the truck. Target another sniper in the small building to the left of the two cars you just sabotaged.

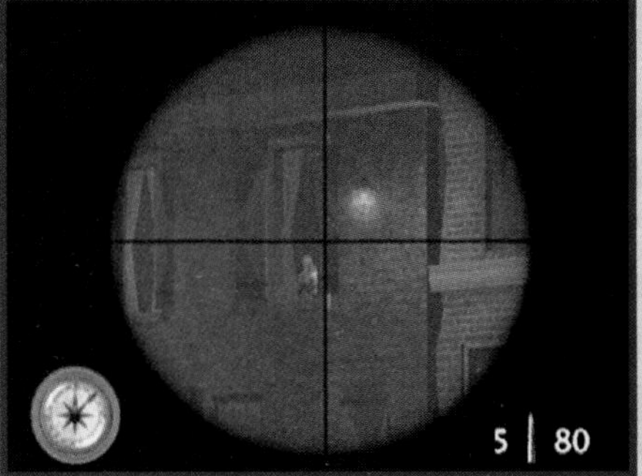

TIP – Low on ammo? Grab the Thompson and Silenced Pistol ammo from the disabled alarm post before boarding the truck.

Cross the courtyard to the final car. Put a fresh clip in the Thompson and scurry along the south side of the courtyard. When you reach the Kubelwagen, open its trunk to complete your work. You've officially disabled the motor pool. Run back to the garage and hop in the truck.

Fox smashes the truck through a roadblock, depositing you in the cathedral courtyard. This area has very little cover, and when you jump down from the truck, you are out in the open. Crouch down and shoot the sentry on the church steps. Enjoy this, your first and last easy shot.

Swing your Springfield to the north and target the alarm station. Move up, hugging the buildings on the left, until you have a clear view of the MG-42. Shoot three guards and then disable the alarm.

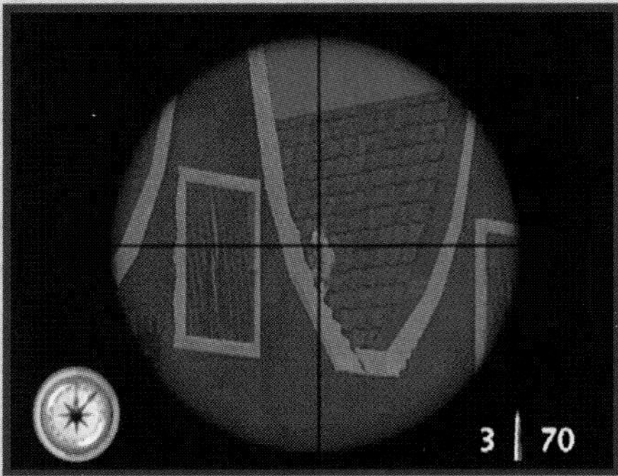

If you haven't already nailed him, take out the sniper on the gabled rooftop to the northwest.

The courtyard should be clear enough to disable the cars. Have your Thompson out and loaded in case a rogue guard rushes up as you clip wires. Remember to open the Kubelwagen's hood for Grenades, Thompson bullets, and a Medical Kit. Disable the last car, then run back to the truck and get ready for another wild ride.

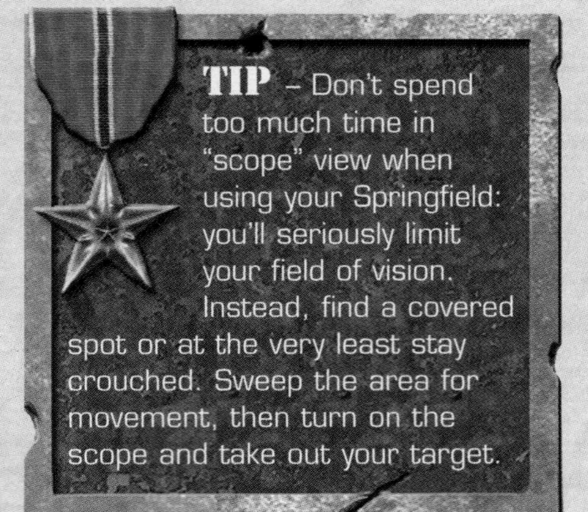

TIP – Don't spend too much time in "scope" view when using your Springfield: you'll seriously limit your field of vision. Instead, find a covered spot or at the very least stay crouched. Sweep the area for movement, then turn on the scope and take out your target.

Next stop: the park, one of the toughest areas in this mission. You encounter four nasty guards, with only a truck for cover. Whirl around and shoot the guard behind you. There's an area under the back of the truck that looks like a perfect spot for shooting the remaining guards. Don't go there! You can fire from here, but your shots will never connect. Instead, back up and give yourself some room.

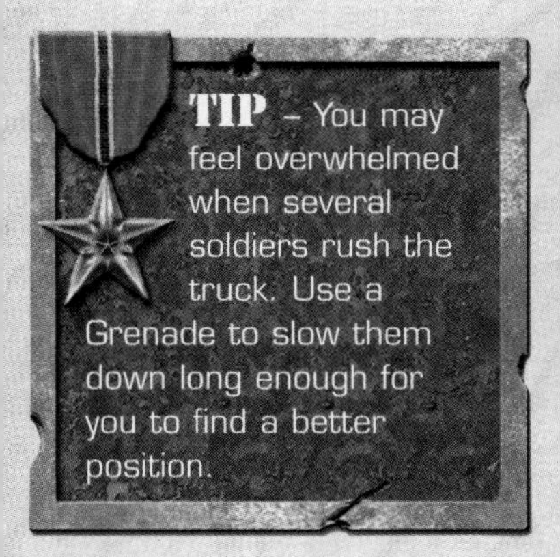

TIP – You may feel overwhelmed when several soldiers rush the truck. Use a Grenade to slow them down long enough for you to find a better position.

Finish with the park guards, then look for the sniper on the roof behind the truck. Back away from the courtyard far enough to see him. Lob several Grenades over the wooden gate to "soften up" your enemies. Remember this step or you will soon run into trouble. Once inside, keep moving; use your Grenades, especially in the northeast corner where several soldiers gather in and around the alcove. Clear this area, then rush into the alcove to gather ammo and a Field Surgeon Pack (you'll need it!).

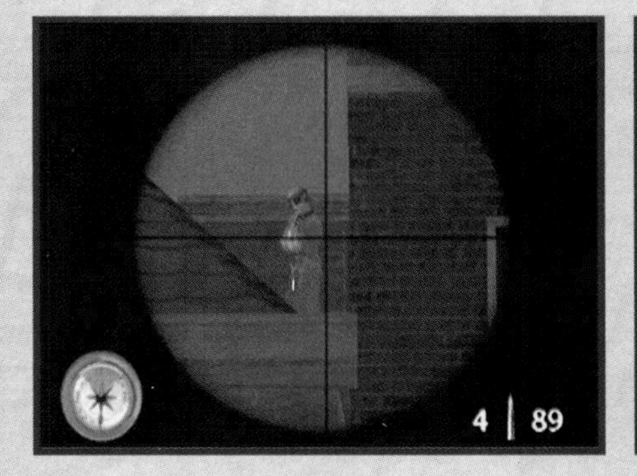

Edge around the corner and take out the last, persistent sniper on the roof to the south. When the shooting stops, run to the gate and remove the bar. Go back to the truck and let Fox drive you to the next location.

GET AN OFFICER'S UNIFORM

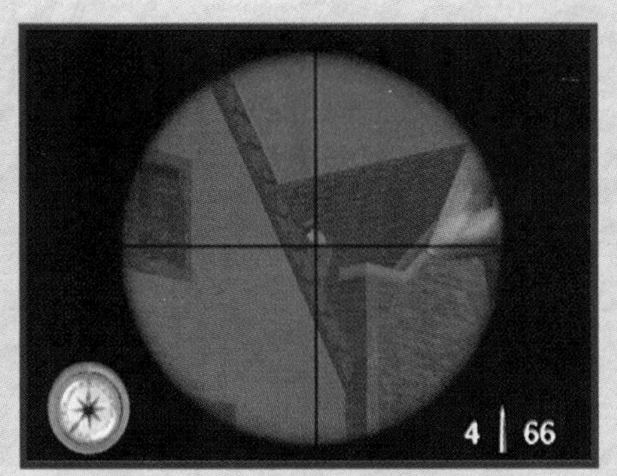

When you arrive in the Mermaid Plaza, go to the delivery truck in the south corner to retrieve a German officer's uniform. Two soldiers guard the truck, and you must neutralize four other soldiers on the ground as well as three elevated snipers. Shoot the guard standing near the truck and then target his partner when he starts running. Swing your rifle to the east, where several soldiers stand clustered around the alarm station. Take them out and then target the sniper on the rooftop above. A second sniper lurks on a rooftop directly behind the mermaid statue.

With the area clear, disable the alarm and gather the ammo and Field Surgeon Pack. Run to the delivery truck and snatch the uniform. The enemy fires as you run. One more sniper perches on a rooftop north of the mermaid statue. After grabbing the uniform, crouch down and move to the northwest corner of the square. Swing your Springfield up and eliminate the final sniper.

Disable the two vehicles, grab the supplies in the Kubelwagen, and head back to the truck. If you need to top off your health, scour the area for health pickups. You'll need every ounce of strength to survive the next checkpoint.

MEET CONTACT IN GOLDEN LION BAR

Fox drives the truck back over the canal bridge until a rocket hits it. In the first screen, you see the Panzerfaust moments before he fires (look to the left of the first lamp post). In the second screen, you see the smoke trail of the rocket. When the truck comes to a rest, you find yourself very close to the railing. You have little time to locate and shoot the Panzerfaust while he reloads, so when you pop up, swing your gun left until you point due north. After taking out the Panzerfaust, swing your Springfield up and shoot the sniper on the roof.

After dispatching the soldiers on the other side of the wooden boxes with a few Grenades, pick up the Field Surgeon Pack and walk north. The last resistance between you and the Golden Lion: two snipers on your left, firing from across the canal as you approach the bridge. Cross the bridge and continue north until you reach a plaza. Walk into the Golden Lion.

As the door opens, you swap your gun for I.D. papers, which means you've donned the German officer's uniform. Walk over to the piano player and press the Action button to ask him to play a song. When he starts playing, the two guards leave their post at the stairs and move to the bar to hear the music. This allows you to walk up the stairs to the left of the bar.

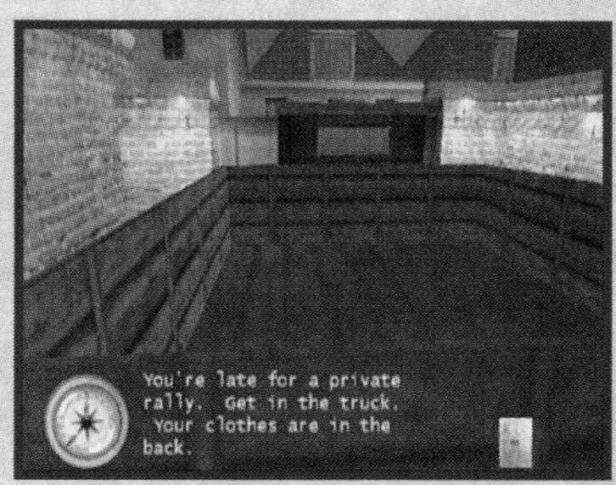

Exit the door at the end of the hallway and walk up to the railing where you see three beers. Press the Action button repeatedly to knock all three beers off the railing. This angers one of the soldiers seated below, prompting a fight. When the two German officers start fighting each other downstairs, walk to the blue door and press the Action button to exit the bar and meet your contact, who tells you to hop into the truck and change your clothes. Your next destination: a private rally. The adventure continues.

OPERATION REPUNZEL

MISSION OBJECTIVES

- Find Kitchen Key Set
- Search the Paintings to Find Map
- Destroy Clocks to Find Documents
- Find Keys to Cell Door
- Locate Gerritt

WEAPONS

- Silenced Pistol
- STG-44
- Shotgun
- Mark II Grenades

FIND KITCHEN KEY SET

Your mission begins in front of Dorne Manor, where you are armed with nothing more than a fake I.D. and a Silenced Pistol. You can walk freely around the grounds without raising suspicion, so don't start popping soldiers until you get inside. As soon as you pass through the side door, your cover is blown, so there will be ample time to demonstrate your marksmanship.

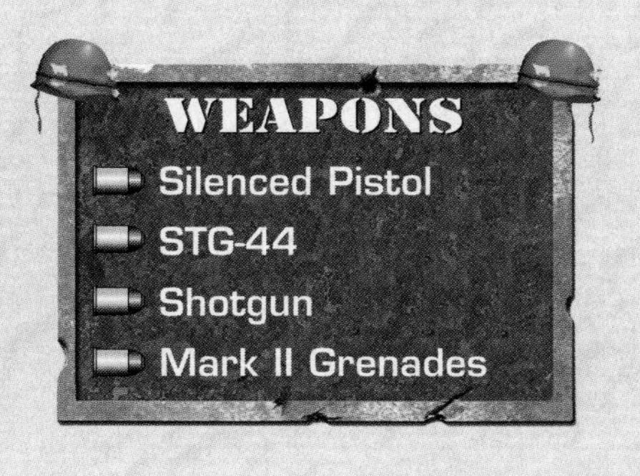

CAUTION – Don't take out your Silenced Pistol until you are inside the mansion. If the guards outside see your weapon, they will attack.

Shoot the guard in the entry area, pick up the shotgun on the crates in the northwest corner of the room, and then continue east down the hall, clearing out the wine cellar on the left.

When you pass the walk-in door on the left, two guards attack you, one straight ahead and another in the foyer off to the right. You can't open the walk-in door until you find the Kitchen Keys, so don't waste your time. You'll probably take a hit or two here, so pick up the Medicinal Canteen in the foyer after the shooting stops.

Your first objective is to find the Kitchen Keys, which are in an office up the stairs. When you reach the room, three soldiers and a civilian attack you. Take out the first guard, then crouch down behind the desk to avoid taking multiple hits. Retrieve the Keys by walking around the corner to the small wooden rack on the wall.

SEARCH THE PAINTINGS TO FIND MAP

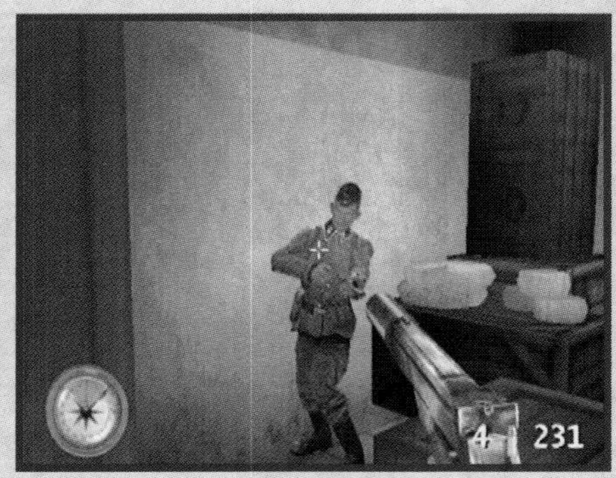

With Keys in hand, go back down the stairs to the walk-in cooler door. Enter and take out the kitchen worker and guard.

Continue down the gray hallway and turn left to enter the laundry room. Take out the soldiers and then edge around the next right-hand corner, which leads to the radio room. Two soldiers shoot at you from a corner at the end of the hallway, so crouch down and hit them as they jump out. Before you leave this area, check out each room for Field Surgeon Packs and a Medical Kit.

Next stop is the kitchen where you find an irritable chef and five workers. Watch out for the chef on the left who launches a barrage of knives in your direction. After taking out the chef, finish off the rest of the staff from long range. When the room is clear, pick up the bread on the tables to replenish your health.

Exit the kitchen through the double doors in the northeast corner and then head back up behind the doors for cover. The entry to the room is wide open, and if you march in, you come under fire from four workers. After eliminating the enemies from long range, walk the entire length of the stage behind the podium to retrieve Shotgun Shells, two Medical Kits, and Grenades. Grab more shells as you walk toward the stairs.

Walk up the stairs to the main hall and take cover behind the curtains on the right. Two guards walk back and forth in the entry room and you easily shoot them as they pass. More guards rush in from either side, so look both ways when you step out from behind the curtains. You also receive fire from the ballroom. Your Silenced Pistol is amazingly accurate from long range, so keep pluggin' away from the main hall.

If you took out the white-coated workers in the ballroom from long range, a drunken soldier is the only remaining enemy when you enter the room. You can shoot him right away, but it's more fun to watch him stagger around and then fall to the floor in a drunken stupor. When he is snoozing peacefully, go behind the bar to retrieve a Medicinal Canteen and the Shotgun.

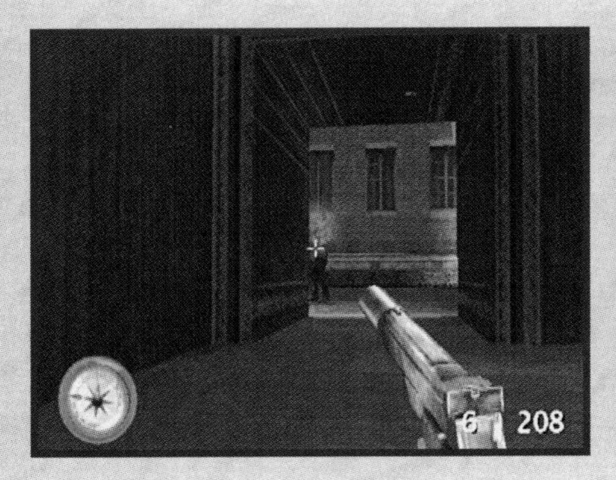

You need your Shotgun to survive the next battle, but for now, keep your Silenced Pistol at your side as you walk towards the garden area. Take out the first two soldiers from long range while you are still inside the ballroom. If you take a few early hits, run back to the ballroom to pick up any health supplies you may have left behind.

There is a much bigger force waiting for you on the patio above and behind you as you enter the garden. Hug the wall to your left, turn around, and aim high as you lob Grenades over the railing. Some of the remaining soldiers will rush down the stairs to the garden. Use your last Grenade to finish them off, or switch to your Shotgun. Continue up the stairs and blast any stragglers. If you survive the garden, you find a Medical Kit and plenty of STG-44 ammo on the stairs and on the second level (you find the STG-44 in the next room).

Go up the stairs and walk to the south end of the corridor to enter the upper gallery of the grand hall. Run to your right and take out the enemy soldiers with your Shotgun as you continue around the gallery and onto the crossover. Don't waste any time here, because there are more enemies on the ground floor, including one who blasts the crossover with a Panzerschreck. If you are unable to make it past the crossover before it is blown up, go downstairs, eliminate the soldiers, and then use the exploded crossover as a ramp back up to the gallery. Before leaving the gallery, find the painting of a ship on the east wall. Press the Action button to look behind the painting and retrieve the map.

DESTROY CLOCKS TO FIND DOCUMENTS

TIP – Pick up the STG-44 located on the podium in the grand hall.

Enter the clock hall at the north end of the gallery, where you find several soldiers and civilians. Don't rush through these three rooms; hang back and take out the enemies as they appear.

Climb the staircase at the end of the clock hall to reach the library. This is as good a time as any to show off your new STG-44. This gun is powerful and accurate, and the 30-shot clip lets you spend more time shooting and less time reloading. Spray the upper area of the library, and then continue up the stairs to clean out the remaining soldiers. Watch for a civilian hanging around in the north corner of the lower level.

The door in the east corner of the library leads into a long hallway. Bypass the first doorway on the left and continue to the game room. Stay in the hallway and ease your way towards the doorway to pick off the uniformed soldier and four more who are lounging in smoking jackets. When the room is clear, shoot the small cuckoo clock on the north wall to the left of the pool table.

FIND KEYS TO CELL DOOR

Go back to the wet room, the first room you passed in the hallway. Depending on how much noise you made in the game room, two German soldiers clad in white bathrobes may inch out into the hallway to confront you, so be ready with a loaded Shotgun or Silenced Pistol. Take care of the enemies in the outer area, then move into the steam room and neutralize the two remaining Germans. Walk up to the dial and press the Action button to reveal a secret passageway.

Walk through the passageway to reach the Resistance HQ. Gather the supplies and walk up the curved staircase.

The staircase leads to the back of a bookcase. To enter the room, press the Action button to slide aside the bookcase. Walk to the other bookcase, which also reveals a secret passageway. Continue to the end (passing the room on the left), and turn left to reach the last secret door. But don't open the door until you read the next section!

CAUTION – The next room is loaded with soldiers. Arm yourself with a Grenade while walking to the end of the passageway.

You're getting near the end, and surviving the master bedroom is the first of two nearly impossible challenges. When the secret door opens, you receive heavy fire from every direction. Don't try and shoot through the paper screen in front of you. You'll be dead by the time you kill one soldier. Instead, lob Grenades over the screen and to the right. When the shooting decreases, or stops, switch to your STG-44 and clean up the remaining soldiers. When the smoke settles, the floor is littered with ammo and health pickups.

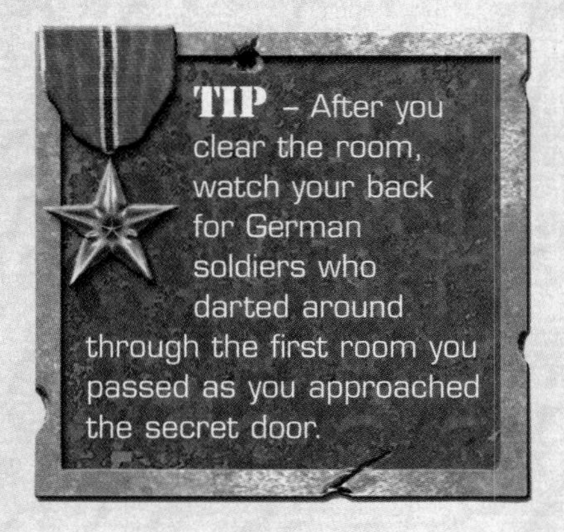

TIP – After you clear the room, watch your back for German soldiers who darted around through the first room you passed as you approached the secret door.

When the master bedroom is clear, move to the adjoining room and eliminate any remaining German soldiers. Search the floor for the Keys and then go back to the master bedroom and open the locked door in the southeast corner of the room. Gerritt will rise to meet you; he shouldn't follow you just yet, so don't press the Action button.

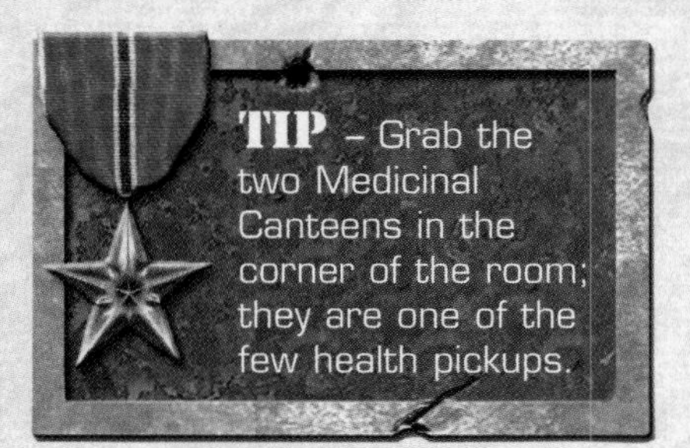

TIP – Grab the two Medicinal Canteens in the corner of the room; they are one of the few health pickups.

LOCATE GERRITT

Return to the adjoining room and take the staircase to the rooftop garden. This is another well-guarded area, and it requires an initial Grenade attack, followed by some accurate strafing with your STG-44 (if you have ammo left). Aside from the soldiers in the garden, there are two nasty snipers on the clock tower. Stay at the perimeter of the garden and inch around until you have a good view of the clock tower and of the two snipers on either side of the clock.

With the garden and rooftops free of enemy soldiers, go back and summon Gerritt to follow you back to the garden. Walk to the outer arcades; move up to the lattice on the south end, and press the Action button to destroy the lattice and motivate Gerritt to jump onto the hay wagon below (actually, he gets a friendly little nudge). Follow him down and then walk to the Kubelwagen to commandeer the vehicle and complete a very tough mission.

SEVERAL BRIDGES TOO FAR

NIJMEGEN BRIDGE

MISSION OBJECTIVES

- Defuse Charges under Bridge
- Destroy Antiaircraft Gun
- Escape in Medical Supply Truck

WEAPONS

- Silenced Pistol
- MP-40
- Gewehr 43

DEFUSE CHARGES UNDER BRIDGE

After receiving instructions from an American soldier, turn around and walk up the cement stairs. Don't go too fast—take out the two guards before they see you. Use your Silenced Pistol to hit the one on the right first. Swing left and take out the second guard. Sprint up the stairs and collect two new weapons (the MP-40 and the Gewehr 43), rounds for each weapon, and a Medical Kit.

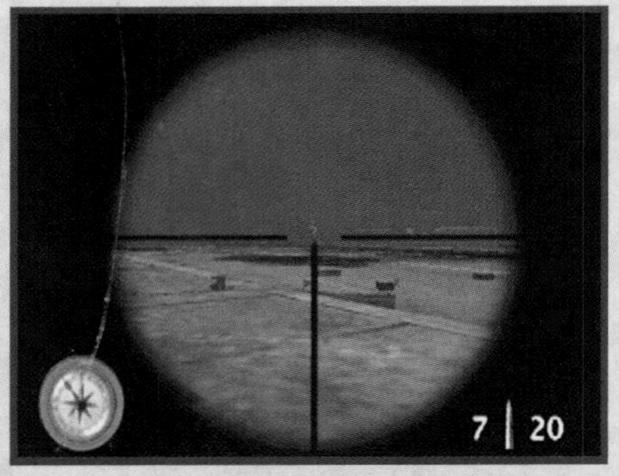

Take out the Gewehr 43 and advance north. Stop when you see two guards advancing on the other side of the road, and take them out from long range. Gewehr 43 lacks traditional crosshairs, so it may take a few shots to get used to the German sight.

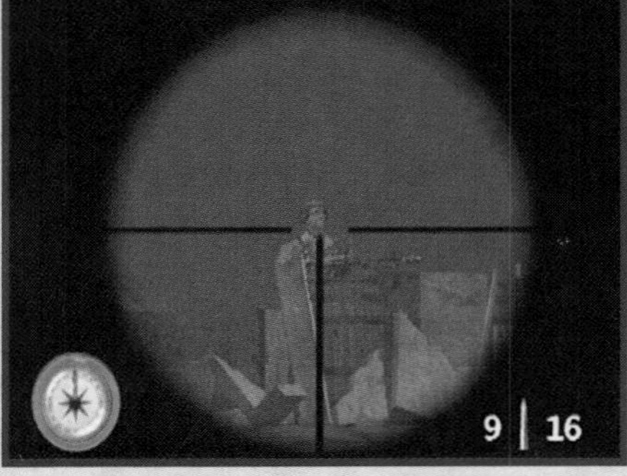

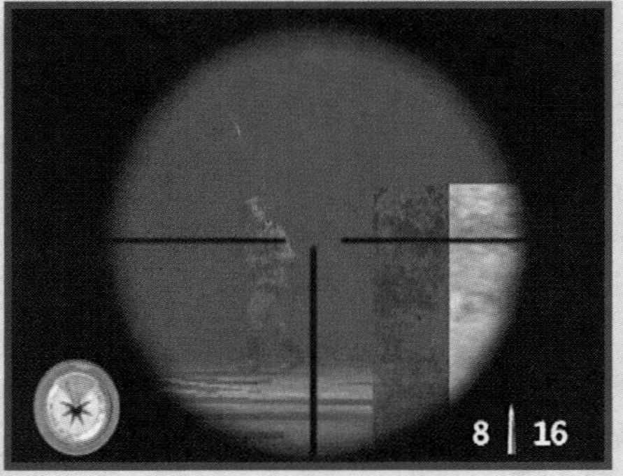

Advance slowly past the burning wreckage until you see the machine-gun nest. Note the guard pacing to the right. After you squeeze off the first shot, you also receive fire from a sniper lying on the pavement. After the last man falls, race to the machine-gun nest and take over the gun.

Aim the machine gun at the top of the stairs where several German soldiers emerge. Aim low.

After the last soldier is on the ground, walk down the stairs. Shoot the soldier who is standing. By the time the other soldier stands up and turns around, you have a bullet in his chest. Defuse the Dynamite that is strapped to the overhead girder, and continue along the bridge. Seven more to go!

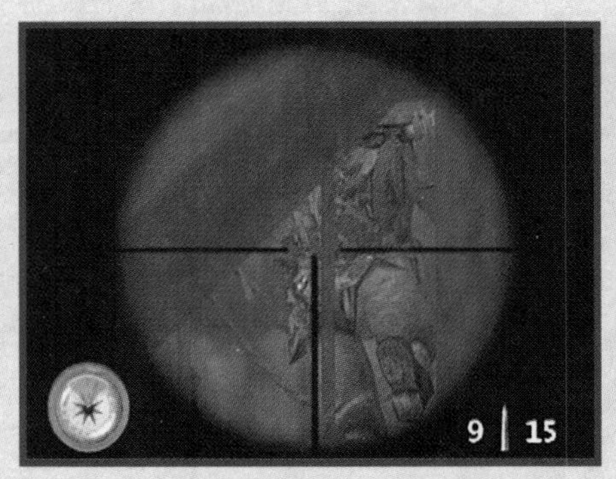

Defuse two charges at this location. The bridge supports make sniping the German soldiers more difficult. After you defuse the second charge, the soldiers see you, so acquire your targets quickly. After taking out the soldiers ahead, defuse the third charge.

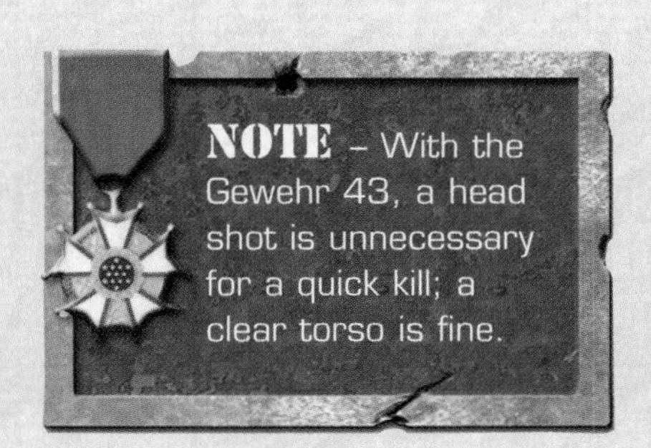

NOTE – With the Gewehr 43, a head shot is unnecessary for a quick kill; a clear torso is fine.

Defuse another charge on the vertical beam ahead, then retrace your steps back to the bridge. When you reach the top, crouch down and look to the right. There are three German soldiers, one standing, two on the ground. Shoot the one standing and then take out the other two. Pick up the discarded ammo, and walk into the wooden shack to collect a Medical Kit.

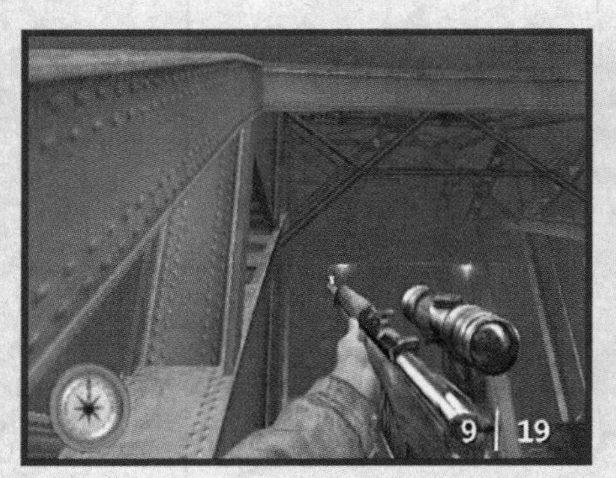

Walk slowly to the north. There is an ambush ahead, including elevated snipers. Look skyward, past the first string of overhead lights. Take out two of the snipers from here, even though they're tough to see. Move behind the last square cement block. Back up slightly and swing the Gewehr up to shoot the third sniper.

Get higher because the other snipers are well hidden. Move along the right side of the bridge. When the ambush ahead fires at you, take cover behind a beam; use your Gewehr to shoot the four soldiers in the center of the bridge.

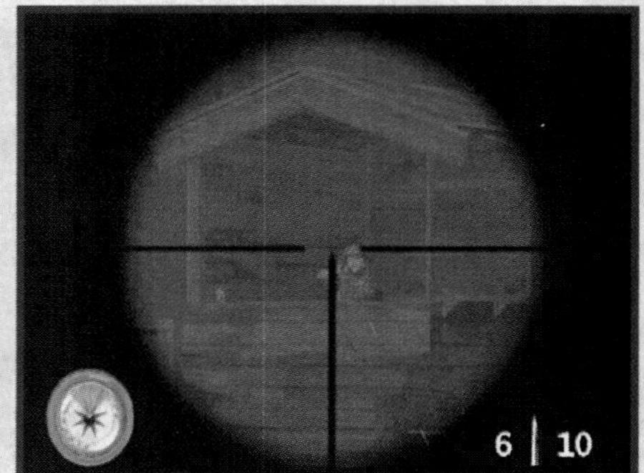

Take out your MP-40 and advance along the right side of the bridge until you see a burned-out truck, which is in front of a ladder. Climb to the top and take out the snipers. Watch out for one more sniper on a catwalk—he's below your position at the top of the ladder. If your health is slipping, look for a Medical Kit on the corner of the southwest girder.

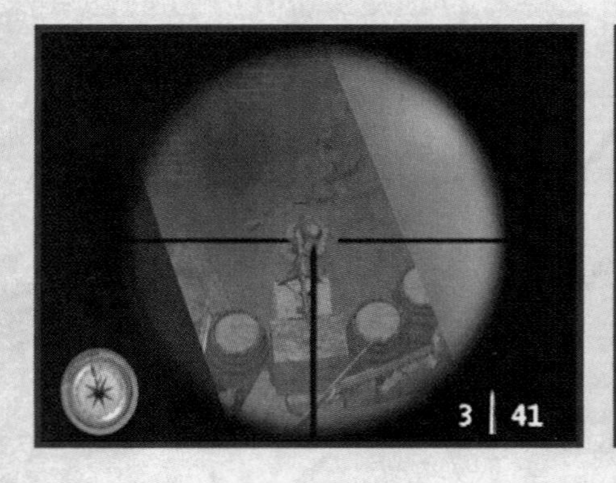
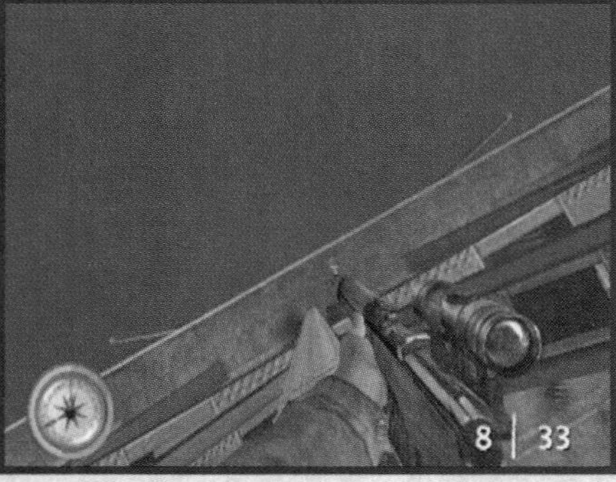

You now have a serious advantage over the remaining German soldiers on the bridge below. Find positions on both sides of the bridge and fire through the slots at the machine-gun nests below. The Germans repeatedly man the positions, allowing you to take out several soldiers without moving your gun. Crawl around the bridge and pick off any soldiers who fire at you. They have a slim chance of hitting you, so move freely, draw fire, and take them out. When all is quiet, climb down to the bridge. Pick up a bushel of ammo at each of the machine-gun nests.

CAUTION – Be careful coming down the ladder; a slip means instant death. The ladder is located in the middle of the bridge on the eastern side. When you get close to the bottom, watch out for one or two surviving soldiers who rush the base of the ladder.

Continue north to the end of the bridge, but watch out for three more sentries, one manning a machine gun. Pick up the Field Surgeon pack in one of the circular cutouts, and gather the dropped ammo. The stairs on the northeast side take you back under the bridge, where you find the remaining charges.

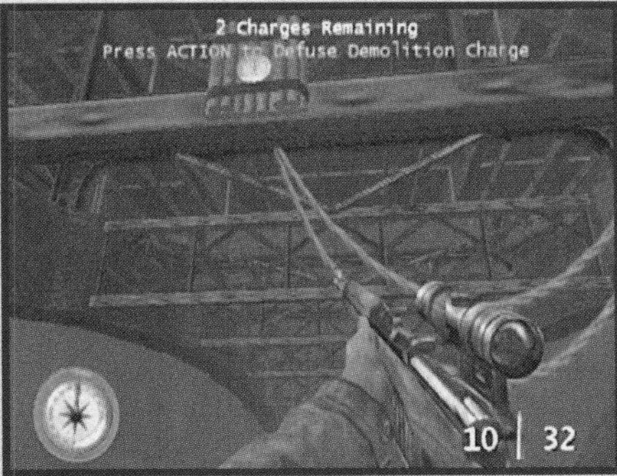

Three soldiers are working on the next charge. When you kill them, disable the charge and advance very carefully, because you come under fire from the catwalk to the north. As you advance down toward the catwalk, look up to defuse the next charge. Two more to go.

Continue along the catwalk until you spot the soldier working on a charge. Shoot him, then swing your gun to the left to take out his buddy. Look for the seventh charge overhead as you climb the stairs. The final charge is just ahead to the left of the toolbox on a vertical beam.

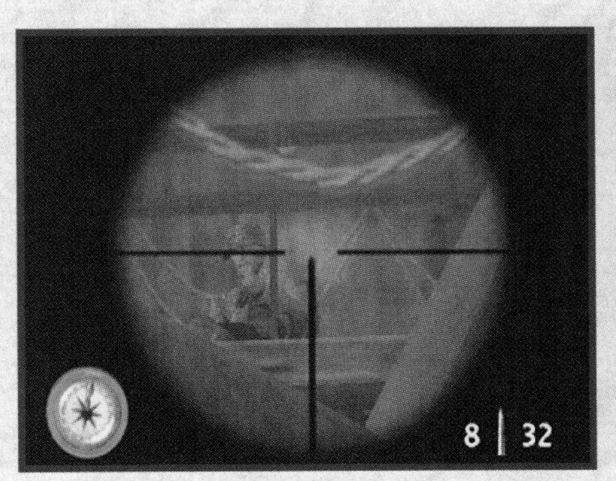

DESTROY ANTIAIRCRAFT GUN

Climb the stairs back up to the bridge and get ready for another ambush to the right. You can take out the early attackers with the Gewehr, but when they start rushing you, switch to the MP-40. When all seems quiet, there is one more German soldier in the wooden shed. Kill him and collect the Medical Kit and his leftover ammo.

Continue north down the road, armed with your MP-40. Three German soldiers suddenly come at you, so get ready for a close-quarters fight. When you reach the roadblock, collect the Medical Kit, turn right, and follow the road as it winds down and around.

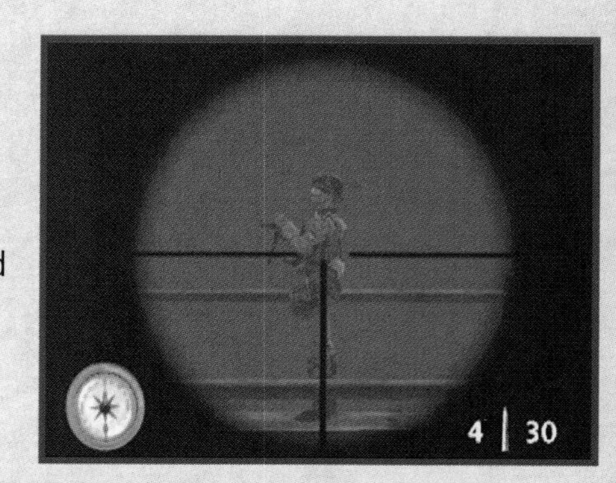

When you hear a truck up ahead, look out for two patrolling guards. When you shoot them, another soldier rushes in from the left. Turn right and collect a Medicinal Canteen and discarded ammo, then proceed east toward the bunker.

You encounter two guards near the bunker, and a third joins the fight when you attack. These soldiers are aggressive and elusive, so use your MP-40. After dispatching them, move cautiously toward the bunker and wait for two more guards to appear.

There's more trouble inside the bunker as you follow the wall around to the right.

Continue up the stairs until you see the antiaircraft gun. Crouch down and inch up until you have a shot at the first two soldiers. Pop up and finish the remaining guards.

ESCAPE IN MEDICAL SUPPLY TRUCK

Walk over to the rag hanging on the fuel drum, and press the Action button to light it on fire. Back away from the impending explosion. You destroyed the gun; now run down the ramp to the supply truck. A German soldier blocks your path, but don't engage him. Simply run past the truck to finish the mission.

YARD BY YARD

MISSION OBJECTIVES

- Clear Enemy Checkpoints from Main Road
- Destroy Radio
- Find Your Way to Central Arnhem

WEAPONS

- Silenced Pistol
- MP-40
- Gewehr 43

CLEAR ENEMY CHECKPOINTS FROM MAIN ROAD

From your opening position, walk across the street and through the brown door. You may draw fire from the checkpoint, but don't return it. Walk up the stairs with your Silenced Pistol drawn and take out the German soldier who is standing at the MG-42. Grab the gun and ravage the German guards on the street below. Be sure and shoot the red gas can to blow up everything and officially destroy the checkpoint.

There is a Medical Kit in the bathroom, but ignore it for now (unless you shot it out with the guards while on the street). Go downstairs with your MP-40 and kill the three soldiers. They all fire at once, so you'll probably take a few hits. Go around the shelves to the counter and eat the three loaves of bread for a nice boost. If you still need more health, go back to the bathroom for the Medical Kit.

Exit the bakery and turn right, but get ready for two German soldiers armed with MP-40s at the end of the street. Take them out and turn left into the passageway. Wind your way around until you reach an alley. Go to the end of the alley (a cart blocks your way) and open the gate on your right. Two German soldiers lounge by the door, but you surprise them and quickly dispatch them.

Enter the kitchen and shoot the soldier standing at the end of the hallway. Dart to the left into the dining room. The German soldiers keep firing at the kitchen, so sneak up behind them and take out at least two before they respond. If you get injured during the fight, grab the bread on the kitchen table before you go upstairs.

At the top of the stairs, enter the room on the right. Pick up the Gewehr bullets in the closet, then crawl through the wooden vent on the left. When you reach the next house, turn right and walk through the door. Take over the MG-42, kill the soldiers, and destroy the second checkpoint.

Exit the room and immediately crouch down to look for German soldiers on the first floor. You can shoot two or three of them from here. Continue down the stairs and finish them off. Collect the discarded ammo and the loaf of bread in the kitchen. Exit the back door and open the gate; German soldiers harass a Dutch civilian. Kill the soldiers and continue into the covered alley across the street.

CAUTION – If you venture down the street to your left, you'll run into three more German soldiers, including a machine-gun nest that is very destructive.

At the end of the alley, go through the wooden gate and into the house. Take the bread and continue upstairs. A civilian opens an overhead crawl space and drops a box of Grenades down to you. Grab them and proceed through the wooden vent door to the next house.

When you emerge from the vent, crawl into the room and kill the soldier standing at the window. Grab the MG-42 and lay waste to the checkpoint below. When all is quiet, remain at the gun until a tank rolls by, and destroy it with the MG-42.

Release the gun and turn to face the German soldier firing at you from the hallway. Kill him and continue downstairs where you find his buddy. Two more soldiers rush in through the kitchen. Finish them off, have a chunk of bread, and head outside. Pick up the Medical Kit and ammo in the yard, then turn left into the covered alley.

When you exit the alley, you see German soldiers harassing another Dutchman. Kill them, then turn left to enter another alley. Two more soldiers race around the corner. Kill them, take their discarded ammo, and destroy two wooden crates on the south side of the street to find more Gewehr ammo and a Medicinal Canteen.

Continue east, almost to the end of the road, and turn left into a new alley. Open the gate on the right and enter the house to find three German soldiers on the ground floor. Go upstairs and into the bedroom. Kill one more soldier and then crawl through the wooden vent into the next house.

After exiting the vent, go into the bedroom on the right and destroy the final checkpoint. Quickly turn around, because the noise alerts the soldiers downstairs. Fight your way to the backyard, kill the last soldier, then head out the gate and into the alley. Collect the health pickups in the yard.

DESTROY RADIO

At the end of the alley, two more German soldiers harass a citizen. Kill them, then jump on the MG-42 to take out another tank. Destroy the tank before it swings its gun turret in your direction. Watch out for a German soldier to your left; he shoots at you while you zero in on the tank.

Continue west down the alley, and duck into the yard on the right. Climb over the ladder into the next yard. A member of the Dutch resistance motions for you to follow. He steps out into the alley, but dies in a hail of bullets. You're on your own. Make your way down the alley, dodging bullets all the way until you reach the last door on the right. Eliminate the guard, enter the house, and destroy the radio command post.

FIND YOUR WAY TO CENTRAL ARNHEM

Incinerate the radio, go back to the alley, turn right, and go up the stairs. Fight your way through the resident soldiers, take two lefts, and go through two doors to reach safety—and the end of the mission.

ARNHEM KNIGHTS

MISSION OBJECTIVES

- Destroy Panzer Tanks and Neutralize Panzerschreck Squad
- Meet Jigs at Customs House

WEAPONS

- Silenced Pistol
- B.A.R.
- Gewehr 43
- Shotgun
- Mark II Grenades

DESTROY PANZER TANKS AND NEUTRALIZE PANZERSCHRECK SQUAD

As the mission begins, you are in another part of Arnhem where the fighting is intense. Walk down the stairs and turn right to meet up with Master Sergeant Kelso, who briefs you on the situation. You must help Kelso's men evacuate the city; along the way, they provide support as you work your way to a new contact. Sprint across the street and up the stairs, where two German snipers inflict serious damage on the Allied troops below. Take them out, and turn your attention to snipers in the building across the street and enemy troops below. More German soldiers rush in from the right. Stay in your elevated position until you kill them all. If you try and fight it out at ground level, you'll take considerable damage.

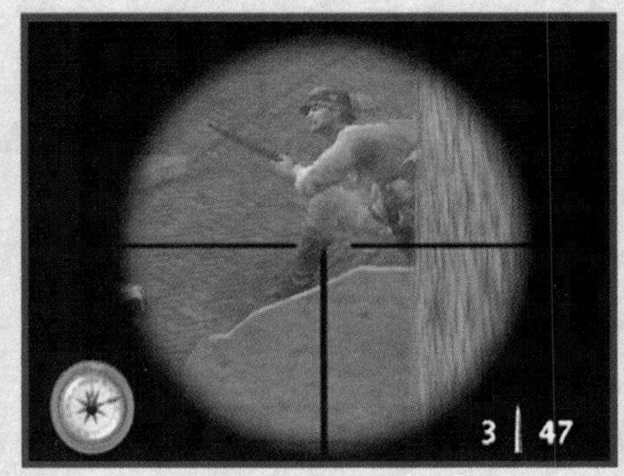

Exit the building and look to the northwest for a wide range of targets. Watch out for rooftop snipers and other German soldiers hiding behind the rubble. As you clear the way, continue moving north, through the remains of a bombed-out building.

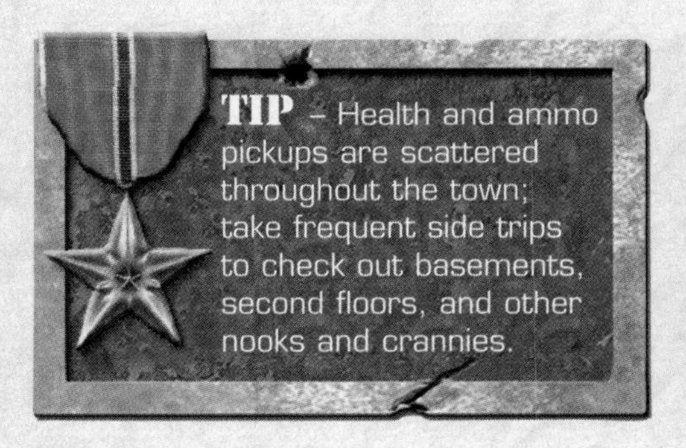

As the street turns toward the southwest, you see an approaching Panzer tank. Find cover on the right side of the street and continue working on the German troops hiding up ahead. The tank will likely see you and start firing. A direct hit is devastating, but even a shell that explodes in front of you can inflict damage, so be careful. Eliminate the German soldiers in front of you, then poke your head out and watch the tank. When the turret swings away from you, rush to the MG-42 and start blasting. As the tank smolders, check the surrounding area for remaining enemy troops. Gather the health and ammo pickups. Take the Field Surgeon Pack behind the remnant of a wall in the southeast corner of the bombed-out building.

When the area is clear and your health and ammo are restored, walk south until you reach an alleyway on the west side of the street. Follow this path to a huge bomb crater, where sniper fire pins down Allied soldiers. German soldiers infest this area, so explore every level and every room on both sides of the street.

Follow the alley to the next street, then walk northwest until you see another nasty fight. Kelso's men take a beating from a German Panzerschreck squad. The Allied troops, however, take out half the squad. The rest is up to you. On your immediate left, walk to the top of the stairs. Look out for one of the Panzerschreck soldiers coming up behind you. Your priority is to take out the MG-42 in the corner of a bombed-out building, north of your position. The Germans reinforce the gun several times, so be patient. When the gun is finally silent, look for the Panzerschreck squad and take them out one at a time. They fire their rockets at you, but you have plenty of time to take them out during reloading. When the enemy squad is history, pick up the Panzerschreck and a bunch of discarded rockets.

Gather every ounce of health you can find; you'll need it to get through the next battle. Move northwest along a narrow rubble-filled street. As you approach the next street, you receive heavy fire from the north (from an MG-42); there are several German soldiers, and just for grins, a Panzer tank. Crouch down and run to the rubble pile on the right side of the street. Lob several Grenades high and far over the pile. Watch out for a potato masher coming back at you. Then, run back to the alcove on the left. Pick off a few German soldiers who venture out in response to your grenade attack.

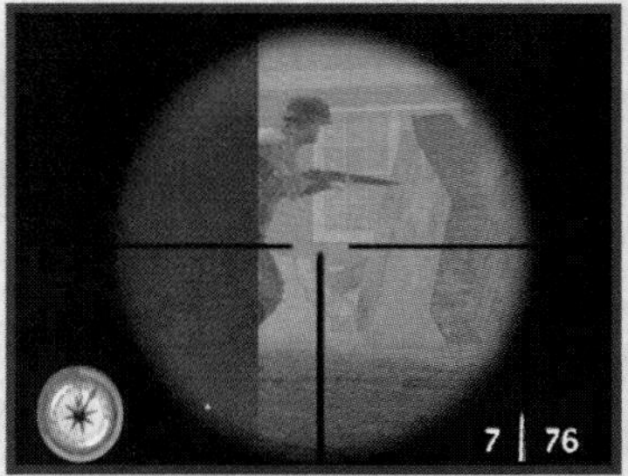
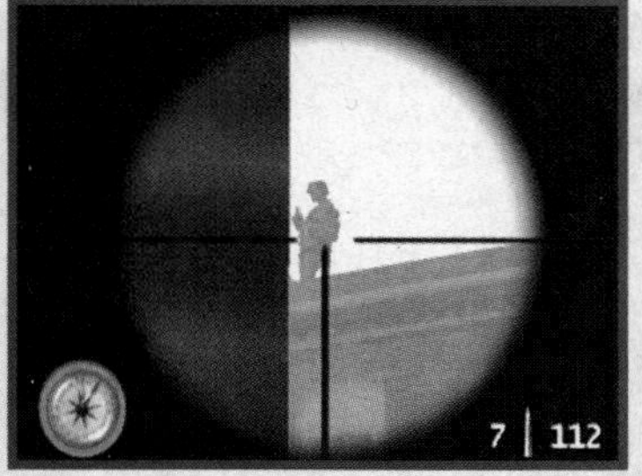

CAUTION – Do not rush the machine-gun nest early in the battle or they'll cut you to shreds. Be patient, change positions frequently, and pick off the enemy soldiers one at a time. Use Grenades as a change of pace and to keep enemy soldiers from swarming you.

Thin out the enemy a little, and run across the street to the shelter of the alcove. More German soldiers rush you, so stay crouched and be ready. Go to the back of the alcove, sweep your Gewehr up to the sky and look for a deadly sniper on the right-hand rooftop.

The MG-42 is deadly. Edge around corners to find a spot where you can fire at the gunners without them seeing you. There are very few angles where you can do this, so you'll need to combine your sniper sessions with Grenades to silence the gun.

The trick to avoiding and eventually destroying the tank is to keep moving, especially after you toss a Grenade or fire the Panzerschreck. Move up the street, dodge machine-gun bullets, and take a narrow passageway on the right that runs behind a house. Edge slowly to the other side to take a shot at the tank as it circles around. If your health is slipping, race across the street to grab the Medical Kit, but duck immediately behind the remnants of the wall to the left or the tank negates your health boost with one shot. Another option for taking out the tank, pictured here, is to fire your Panzerschreck from the alcove on the left side of the main street. Once again, don't sit in one spot and lob shells or the tank nails you.

MEET JIGS AT CUSTOMS HOUSE

After the tank is disabled, watch out for the remaining German soldiers who attack you from behind the house. Proceed to the customs house. A German soldier is waiting on the second floor of the building to the left of the customs house. Climb the stairs and take him out. Once inside, scale the stairs to the upper floor and walk to the end of the hall. Open the last door on the right to meet your contact and bring this nerve-shattering mission to an end!

ROLLING THUNDER

ON TRACK

MISSION OBJECTIVES

- Steal Officer's Uniform and ID Papers
- Enter Train Station
- Destroy Station Controls
- Board Sturmgeist's Train

STEAL OFFICER'S UNIFORM AND ID PAPERS

As the mission begins, you watch from the balcony of your hotel room as Herr Sturmgeist arrives with his lackeys. After he disappears into the building, enter the hallway to activate your Silenced Pistol. Go down the hall and enter the room on the left, where you find an Officer's Uniform and ID Papers. Tap the Change Weapon button to put your pistol away and activate your stolen ID.

ENTER TRAIN STATION

Go down the stairs, walk through the kitchen, and exit through the door. Show the approaching officer your ID, but don't dawdle. Exit the hotel and walk to your left, toward the train station.

Flash your ID to the man standing on the steps, but rather than wait for a response, walk up to the door and turn around. You see "Captain Underpants" arriving on the scene to implicate you as the man who stole his ID and uniform. Your cover is blown, and the ID Papers automatically change to the Silenced Pistol. Shoot the guards closest to you, then run through the doors and into the train station. Run down the main hall and open the door to the left of the ticket windows.

DESTROY STATION CONTROLS

Make sure your pistol has a fresh clip, then exit the ticket office through the door to your right. Two guards lounge in the baggage room. If you move quickly, you can rush in and pound them into submission with the butt of your pistol. If not, two head shots will work just as well. One of the guards drops an MP-40, and you find ammo in the room. Don't miss the MP-40, because you've almost exceeded your pistol's usefulness in this mission.

Walk downstairs to the laundry room, where two guards with MP-40s wait for you. Take them out, pick up the discarded MP-40 ammo, and grab the Medicinal Canteen near the steam presses.

A doorway on the south side of the room leads to a staircase that takes you to the control room. At the top of the stairs, neutralize the German officer who has his back to you, then whirl to the right to face another soldier by the desk, plus one more who races in from the hallway. With the room clear, lay waste to both sides of the control panel. You've probably absorbed some punishment, so get the Medical Kit next to the filing cabinets on the north wall. Before you leave the control room, check the staircase for German soldiers sneaking up from behind.

BOARD STURMGEIST'S TRAIN

Exit the room through the west door and turn left. At the end of the hall, open the door on the right side to enter the kitchen. Guess who's come back for more? Your old buddy, the knife-wielding chef. Kill him, then grab two slices of bread on the counter for a quick health boost.

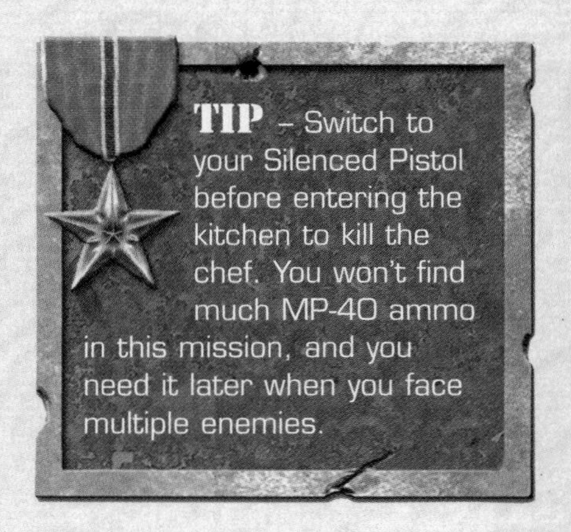

TIP – Switch to your Silenced Pistol before entering the kitchen to kill the chef. You won't find much MP-40 ammo in this mission, and you need it later when you face multiple enemies.

The next door leads into the lounge, where several German soldiers occupy a table on the far side of the room. Use a Steil Grenade to take out at least two of them, then finish off the survivors with a short burst from your MP-40. Turn to the right and eliminate the bartender and another German soldier. When the smoke clears, pick up the MP-40 ammo and a Medicinal Canteen.

A small waiting room attached to the bar leads to a catwalk overlooking the train station. If you pause here, you can kill one or two soldiers as they charge into the room. This allows you to replenish your MP-40 ammo before stepping onto the catwalk. Turn left and run south towards the stairs, taking out any Germans in your path.

Run down the stairs and across the tracks to a fenced storage area. Kill the three German soldiers (two hide behind the wooden boxes), then gather a Medical Kit and Field Surgeon Pack, along with dropped ammo.

Before you exit the cage, scan the area for any German soldiers you can shoot from your covered position. Run up the stairs on your right to pick off any soldiers firing from the catwalk or across the tracks. You can also run back and forth across the tracks, using the train for cover, to blast the soldiers on the ground. From the catwalk, go down the stairs in front of the cage and move to the far north side of the platform. German soldiers pop out from behind the pillars, but use the same cover. If you can't get a good shot, toss a Steil Grenade down the platform, then move up to eliminate the survivors. Clear your path, then continue to the end of the platform and open the last door on the left.

You encounter at least two German soldiers as you weave your way through the hallway. Stop at the boiler room on the left to pick up a Medical Kit and Steil Grenades.

Go up the stairs, around the corner, and down the hallway to the waiting room. Two German soldiers start firing as soon as you turn the corner. Dispatch them, pick up the Medical Kit, and proceed into the waiting area where you find the last soldier.

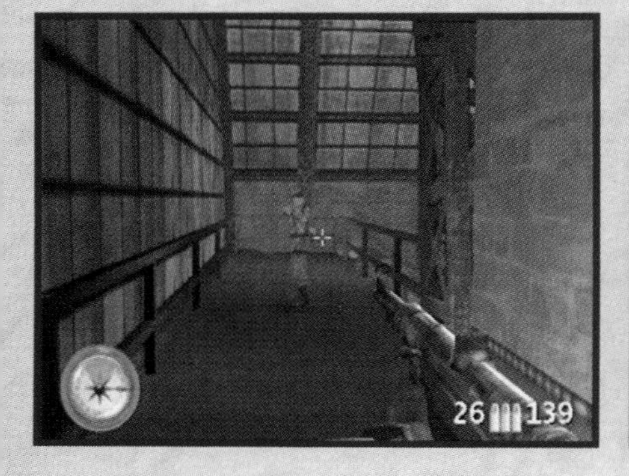

Continue through the next hallway to the second set of tracks. A German guard waits on the catwalk but he's an easy mark. Move toward the stairs and watch for an enemy soldier hiding behind the brick pillars below.

Walk north along the tracks, using the pillars for cover. As you approach the end of the platform, several German soldiers pop out from the door on the left and others appear from across the tracks. Avoid a shootout, or you die here. Stay behind the pillars and acquire your targets. If you can't get the upper hand, toss a Steil Grenade down the platform. Pick up the discarded ammo and exit through the door on the left.

Go up the stairs to the door at the end of the hallway. Several enemy soldiers occupy the cargo office, including two waiting right behind the door. Make every shot count here, because your health may be seriously low at this point. Secure the room and collect two Medical Kits and an assortment of ammo.

The cargo office connects to the cargo room, which teems with enemy soldiers. They can see you through the windows. Shoot out the windows and toss a few Grenades down below before you exit the room. A tough fight still lies ahead. Stand at the windows and snipe, or step out onto the catwalk and shower the Germans with bullets and Grenades. Either way, take out as many soldiers as possible before descending into the cargo room.

Go to the end of the catwalk and scurry down the stairs. Find cover behind the boxes and assess the number of enemies still in the room. Circle around and pick off the German soldiers until you sweep the room clean.

Exit the green double doors on the north side of the cargo room, but watch out for guards on the other side. Sturmgeist's train lies ahead; board the flatbed car at the south end of the station. Hop onto the car to finish the mission.

RIDING OUT THE STORM

MISSION OBJECTIVES

- Destroy Radio
- Hunt Down Sturmgeist and Steal His Briefcase

WEAPONS

- Walther P-38
- STG-44
- Steil Grenades
- Panzerschreck

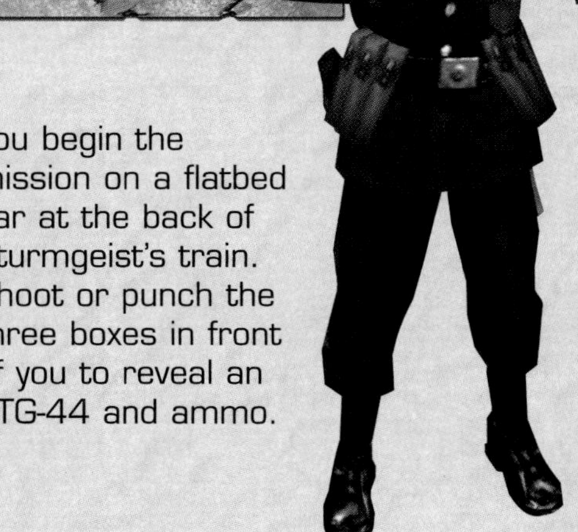

DESTROY RADIO

You begin the mission on a flatbed car at the back of Sturmgeist's train. Shoot or punch the three boxes in front of you to reveal an STG-44 and ammo.

Move quickly across the next two cars, a flatbed and a tank car, and open the door to the fourth car. Don't stop to look at that scout car firing at you from the track to the right.

Once inside the turret car, do away with the two German soldiers, then climb the ladder at the front of the car. Press the Action button to man the gun. Aim at the scout car traveling alongside your train. One hit to the top left section puts it out of commission. Pick up the STG-44 ammo and Medical Kit before moving to the next car.

Use your Walther P-38 to eliminate the two sleeping soldiers in the fifth car, the first of two troop carriers. If you moved quickly through the previous car, you discover them sleeping. However, even if they wake up or get out of bed you can easily kill them.

Load your STG-44 to take care of three machine-gun-toting soldiers in the sixth car. Pick up the ammo discards and the Medical Kit.

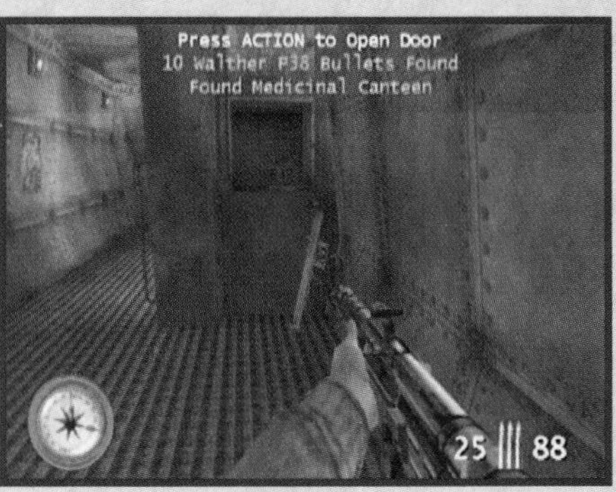

In the seventh car, pick off the lone German soldier sitting at the desk. If someone tipped him off, he's around the corner on the left, midway through the car. Pick up the ammo for the Panzerschreck and Walther, as well as the Medicinal Canteen on the desk.

Load your STG-44, open the car door, and race to the front of the Panzerjager. Fire a few rounds at the soldiers on the next car, then run back into the previous car. Don't stay out in the open for long: a scout car has your number. Crouch down and dust the remaining soldiers who follow you. You likely find one more soldier remaining on the other side of the Panzerjager. Load your STG-44, race across the left side of the Panzerjager, and take out the remaining soldier. Grab a machine gun and lay fire on the scout car until it bursts into flames.

Load your STG-44 and go past the tank carrier to the eleventh car, where you meet two German soldiers armed with machine guns. Collect the STG-44 ammo and Medical Kit.

CAUTION – The scout car perforates you in a major way if you give it more than a second or two, so get behind the machine gun as quickly as possible.

Take out the soldiers in the twelfth car, the troop carrier car, pick up the Field Surgeon Pack and ammo, and move on to the command car. A German officer hides on the left. Shoot him and the radio operator at the end of the car. Destroy the radio to fulfill your first objective.

HUNT DOWN STURMGEIST AND STEAL HIS BRIEFCASE

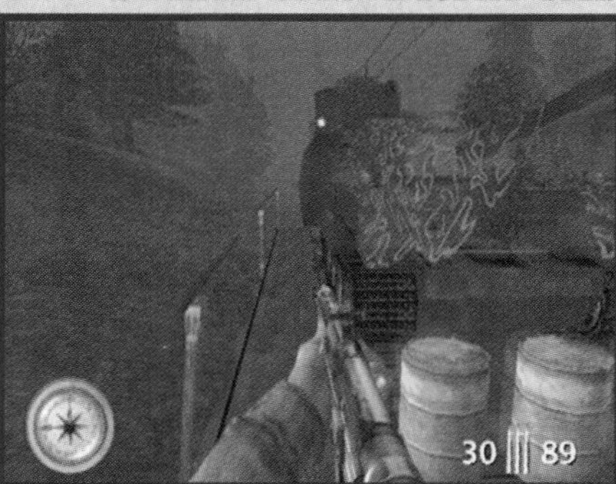

The next two cars carry tanks, and you need them for cover while the scout car on the right thunders at you with its machine gun and tank turret. Stay on the left and work your way to the sixteenth car, a twin-turret gun car. Resist the temptation to go up in the turret or the scout car toasts you.

In an unoccupied boxcar, you see that the eighteenth and nineteenth cars carry two more tanks. You find no enemy soldiers, but the ever-present scout car still seeks your destruction, so use the tanks for cover and move to the next car.

The twentieth car features two Panzer IV tank turrets, one on each end of the car. Take your pick and man the gun to blow up the turrets on the armored train rolling beside you. Keep your eye on the enemy gun turret to succeed here. Fire until the enemy gun turret begins rotating toward you—climb down before it nails you. If you made it down into the car when the shell hits, you avoid taking damage. After the shell lands, climb up and take a couple more shots. When the turret goes up in flames, you've done your job.

One more car to go. Check the clip on your STG-44 and open the door to Sturmgeist's car. Walk past the bed and open the door; Sturmgeist urges his guards to kill you. The guards jump out from behind the door with machine guns blazing. Rake them with your STG-44, then pick up Sturmgeist's briefcase.

Open the next door; Sturmgeist hangs onto the ladder. He unhooked your car for a last second getaway. But have patience. You have a bullet with his name on it.

DERAILED

MISSION OBJECTIVES

- Infiltrate Train Yard
- Find the Demolition Charges
- Destroy Fuel Depot
- Find Transportation to Gotha

WEAPONS

- Walther P-38
- STG-44
- Panzerschreck
- Steil Grenades

INFILTRATE TRAIN YARD

The mission begins on the train tracks, and eventually you work your way west along the tracks. For now, veer to the right on the dirt trail until you see a soldier sitting by a bicycle. If you club him over the head, you get the jump on the three soldiers in the bunker above. You can shoot the lad by the bike, just anticipate a more aggressive attack when you enter the bunker. Take out the soldiers, grab the MG-42, and spray bullets at any remaining enemies below. Collect the ammo and health pickups and go back to the tracks.

Continue west along the right side of the tracks, but beware of any survivors from the first skirmish who might lurk in the bushes ahead. When you see the train car, edge up to see a German soldier at the side door of the car. Shoot him, then get ready to rock. You deal with six more soldiers, including one who loves throwing Steil Grenades in your direction. Rush into the train car, shoot one or two soldiers, then jump out again, looking for more enemies on either side of the car. When the dust settles, go back in the car and gather the ammo, health pickups, and Panzerschreck. Keep moving to survive this fight.

That last battle was a piece of cake compared to the upcoming train yard. Continue along the tracks to a large double door. Load a full clip in your STG-44 and open the door. Note the Medical Kit ahead, but don't go for it! Instead, run to the sandbags on your right and pop the two soldiers who jump up on the other side. Run toward the passageway behind the long building to the north. Along the way, look for a Gewehr; you need it to neutralize the snipers in the yard.

Run to the back end of the building, and kill the soldier at the corner. Turn around just in case another enemy arrives. Sweep your Gewehr to the sky and nail the sniper on the smokestack above. The following sections reveal the locations of the remaining elevated snipers.

This sniper hides on the roof just in front of the smokestack.

Three snipers await you on the tower in the middle of the yard. Two shoot at you while you shoot their colleague, so take excellent cover, such as the long building. Inch out, take a shot, then withdraw.

Another sniper pops up and down in the guard tower to the east. Take cover behind the bushes on the other side of the yard, focus the crosshairs on the ledge of the tower, and nail this nasty boy when he sticks his head up.

You deal with one more sniper at ground level. Take cover around the corner of the building at the south end of the yard. Look north to the large gray building; a German soldier fires through the broken glass.

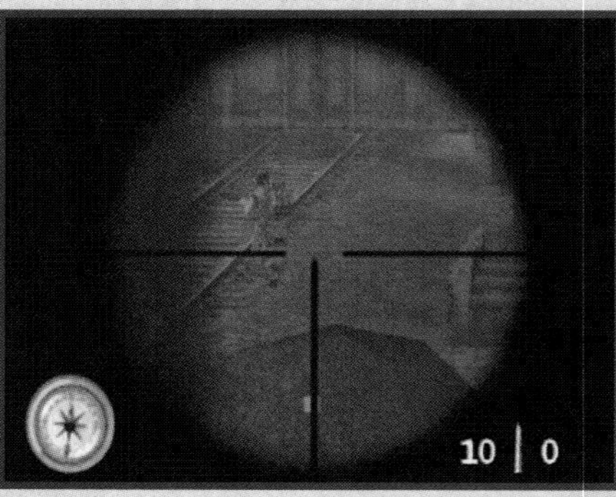

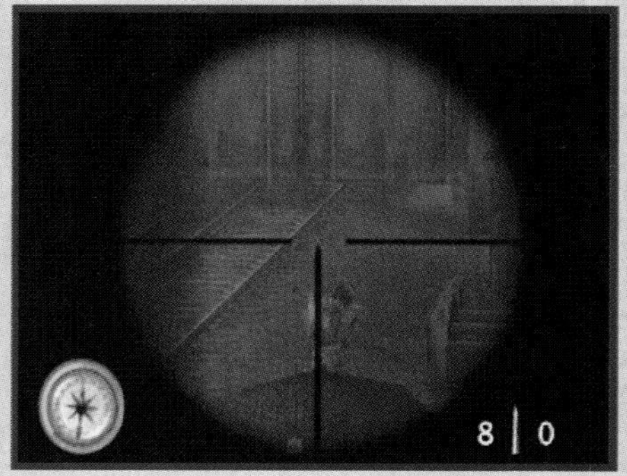

The remaining soldiers move around the yard, three of them armed with Panzerschrecks and rifles. Target them from the balcony of the yard tower, where you sweep the entire yard from east to west. One soldier hangs around the coal piles. If you fire at him and miss, he takes off, unlike some snipers who maintain their positions. Remember, even though an enemy fires at you with a rifle, he still might have heavy artillery. If you see the green tube, take cover, or you take a major hit.

To achieve your goal, advance farther into the train yard. To do this, align the engine track with the turntable. At the top of the yard tower, use the middle switch to align the tracks. Pick up the Medical Kit next to the desk. Depending on how many German soldiers you have already eliminated, you may encounter resistance on your way up. You definitely run into trouble on your way down.

FIND THE DEMOLITION CHARGES

With the tracks aligned, run to the engine barn and press the Action button to hop onto the engine moving down the track. Snipers fire at you along the way, but you don't face serious trouble until the engine stops and tosses you onto the ground.

After you stop, run into the gray building on the right. Approach the stairs, and prepare for a fight. Either toss a Grenade through the door or come up firing. Clear the area, then proceed into the train car and gather a wealth of ammo, a Field Surgeon Pack, and the Demolition Charges.

DESTROY FUEL DEPOT

With Demo Charges in hand, continue down the tracks to reach a large double wooden door. For grins, you can shoot the feet of the German soldiers before setting a Demolition Charge on the door. Back up quickly and pull out your Gewehr for the battle to come.

As you advance, look down the track for several German soldiers. Pay special attention to a sniper on the platform to your left. Walk past the platform, pick up the dropped ammo, and continue toward the next demolition site; watch out for snipers hiding behind the steel towers on the left.

At the end of the platform, look to your left for two large fuel tanks. Place a Demolition Charge on each one, and continue down the track.

Proceed east and use your Gewehr to pick off the sniper in the tower on the left side. Place a Demolition Charge on the third fuel tank located atop a wooden platform. As the fuel depot explodes, fill your STG-44 and get ready for the German soldiers waiting west of the doors.

FIND TRANSPORTATION TO GOTHA

Watch for snipers hiding in the bushes as you walk toward the engine. Climb aboard and press the Action button to start moving.

As the engine picks up speed, you come under attack from both sides of the road. Lead your targets properly and you eliminate several soldiers before you reach the gates. Heavy resistance lies ahead, so any casualties you inflict along the way lessens the opposition.

The engine stops at a barbed-wire gate. Stay alert because German snipers followed the train to its final destination. Stay on either side of the tracks, crouch down, and look for targets through the barbed wire. Clear the immediate area, then proceed through the open gate.

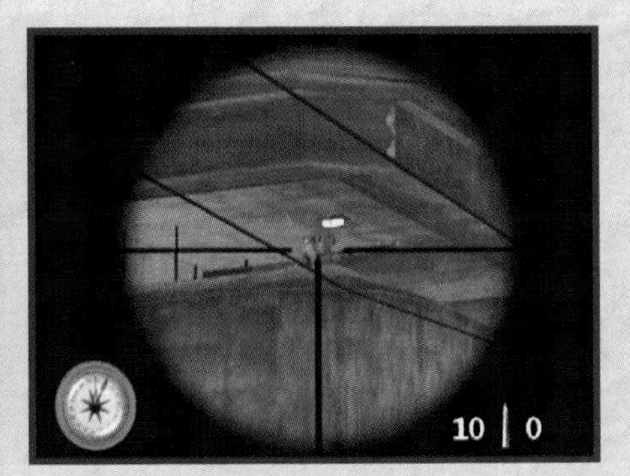

Once again, use your Gewehr to target German soldiers from long range. If you don't thin the ranks before advancing, you fall—just yards from the end of this mission. Two machine-gun nests perched on either side of the track pose your biggest challenges. You only need one shot to silence the one on the right, but the German soldiers reinforce the nest on the left, so stand your ground and wait until you kill three gunners.

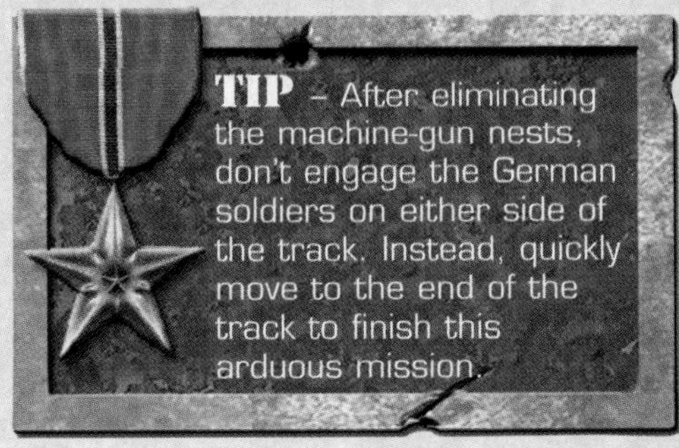

Continue north down the track to reach the engine located before the barbed-wire gate. This takes you to Gotha. Relax. You've finished Derailed!

THE HORTEN'S NEST

CLIPPING THEIR WINGS

MISSION OBJECTIVES

- Find the Weapons Stash
- Find the Spy Camera
- Find the Ammo Room
- Photograph Five Blueprints and Locate the Plans for the HO-IX
- Find a Way into the Manufacturing Plant
- Destroy the Test Engine
- Exit the Facility

FIND THE WEAPONS STASH

You start this mission with only a Walther P-38, which is hardly optimum. The early challenge is staying alive long enough to find the Weapons Stash and ammo room. You begin inside an air duct. Move to the vent and use the Action button to open it. A German agent is in the next room, so take him out before you jump down.

Descend to the ground floor and move toward the office on the south side of the building. As you approach, use your Walther to take out the soldier standing in front of the window. Enter the office, pick up the dropped ammo, and flip the red switch on the north wall to open the garage door.

Enter the garage and hide behind the trucks as you pick off the workers. Enter the office door on the southwest side of the garage, take out the lone guard, and continue into the adjacent room. Collect the Weapons Stash, including a B.A.R., a Gewehr 43, and a Bazooka. Now, all you need are a few bullets!

FIND THE SPY CAMERA

Tiptoe out the east door and shoot the sleeping soldiers in their bunks. The shots awaken the other soldiers; they stand and shoot back as you reach the south side of the room. Open the trunks to gather Medicinal Canteens and Walther bullets; pick up the Spy Camera in a chest located against the south wall.

FIND THE AMMO ROOM

Walk east toward the adjacent room and kill the guard in the doorway. Enter the ammo room and gather ammo for all of your weapons. Load them up before you leave the room!

PHOTOGRAPH FIVE BLUEPRINTS AND LOCATE THE PLANS FOR THE HO-IX

With your B.A.R., proceed north into the dining room; stay behind the columns when you receive fire. Take out the guards, then sneak around the corner to target the knife-wielding chef. Grab the pieces of bread on the counters to replenish your health.

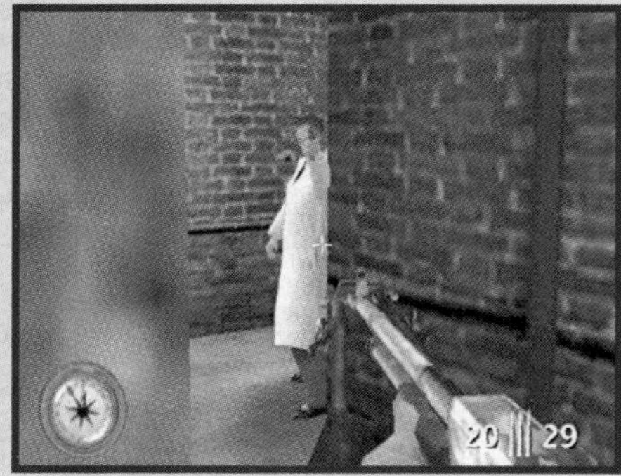

Leave the kitchen and clear out the bricked corridors where you run into guards and scientists. To find out what's around the corner, poke your head out, then immediately step back. If you don't draw fire, the corner is clear.

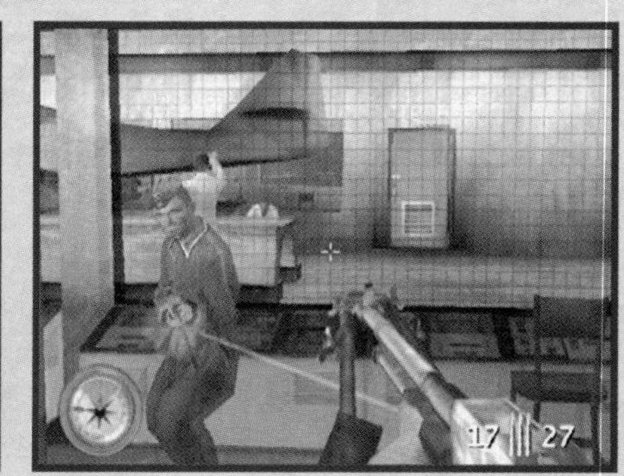

Move toward the wind-tunnel lab entry door, at the eastern end of a short hallway. Take out the guards—one at the door and another inside the control room—and watch out for a scientist who enters from the lab. Now, for some fun. Press the red switch on the control panel to activate the wind machine, which blows the scientists and the jet into the wall.

After the explosion, the door to the wind-tunnel lab swings open. Walk through the wind tunnel to the office on the opposite side. The office is empty, but you find plenty of enemies when you leave through the door in the northern corner of the room.

Clear out the bricked corridors and continue into the lab areas (white tile walls). Shoot the green bottles on the tables to quickly eliminate the lab scientists. The resulting explosion is entertaining and very effective.

Move from lab to lab, eliminating the scientists and guards while taking pictures of the five blueprints on the walls. You find the HO-IX plans rolled up on a desk in the infirmary, a two-room suite. The first room contains, among other things, a table, bed, refrigerator, and washing machine. Continue to the next room to photograph one of the blueprints and collect the HO-IX plans.

FIND A WAY INTO THE MANUFACTURING PLANT

Follow the Ausgang (Exit) signs until you reach an entrance to the catwalk that overlooks the manufacturing plant. Do not rush in! The plant is filled with snipers on all levels, and if you wander out onto the catwalk, your days are numbered. Before you step out, edge up to the right side of the doorway and snipe the welder on the other side of the catwalk. Immediately switch to your B.A.R. and take out the guard who rushes the door from the left. Proceed onto the catwalk with extreme caution; always look for a gun flash to reveal another sniper. Work your way to the lower level, but keep an eye on the upper entrances to the room. New guards arrive at the doors, and they have excellent shooting angles when you are in the middle.

DESTROY THE TEST ENGINE

The Test Engine is located two rooms east of the main plant. Move into the next room and take out the lone sniper in the southeast corner. Continue to the adjacent room, which appears to be empty, except for the Test Engine. Turn right and go up to the control room. Kill the scientist and crank the red lever on the north wall until the needle moves to the far right. Go to the platform above the Test Engine; push the green button to destroy the engine.

After the explosion, watch out for two more angry scientists hanging around on the lower level.

EXIT THE FACILITY

Head north with your B.A.R. fully loaded. Take out two enemies at the beginning of the hallway, and eliminate several more as you head toward the smelting room. The hallways take you back and forth, but your ultimate goal is to reach the north end of the building.

Pull out your Gewehr when you see the opening to the smelting room on the left. This is an exercise in patience as you methodically move around the room on the catwalks, dropping down a level as you clear it. You receive fire from every direction, so avoid rushing out in the open. The fiery smelter casts an eerie glow over the entire room. When you snipe a bad guy, watch him tumble over the railing into the molten steel.

At the furnace room, work your way toward the coal piles, but watch out for snipers popping up from behind the coal and on the overhead catwalk. Take the stairs and catwalk up and over the coal piles to reach the entrance to the mine.

Fight your way to the mine entrance and head east to the beginning of the track to find the exit and finish the mission.

ENEMY MINE

MISSION OBJECTIVES

- Ride Mine Cart to Secret Radar Installation

WEAPONS

- Walther P-38
- B.A.R.
- Gewehr 43
- Bazooka
- Steil Grenades

RIDE MINECART TO SECRET RADAR INSTALLATION

The mission begins where the last one left off, at the entrance to the mine. Before boarding your cart, turn left and pick up the ammo. This is a one-way express trip, so pack everything before leaving the station.

Grab your B.A.R. as the cart rolls toward a wooden barrier. The first of many enemy soldiers appears on the other side of the opening; from here to the end it is like a theme park ride!

Your one real objective on this mission: Be alive at the end! Getting there depends on following a few strategies. First, there are far too many enemy soldiers to shoot one-by-one. Blast every fuel drum possible to create massive explosions that take out several enemies at a time.

There is one exception to the fuel drum strategy: When a soldier hoists a Panzerschreck to his shoulder, shoot him before he pulls the trigger, or you are toast. Because of the Panzerschreck, load your B.A.R. and keep it out for the entire ride. The Bazooka makes a bigger explosion, but it is difficult to aim, and the reload time is brutal on this wild ride.

Gotta love those fuel drums!

Fuel drums on a crowded platform give you the biggest bang for your buck.

This wide-open area is devoid of fuel drums, so marksmanship becomes critical to your survival.

This is the most critical point in the ride. Immediately after picking up the first Medical Kit, focus your aim on the platform ahead and to the right, where the Germans fire a big gun from a cement bunker. Hit the fuel drums to blow up the platform before the gun fires, or you are blown back to the starting line.

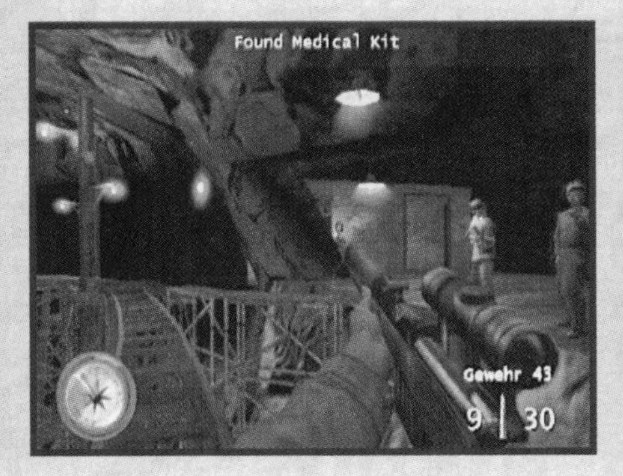

Survive the rest of the way by picking off a variety of individual targets. Sadly, the fuel drums are all but gone. Look for snipers perched above the track.

As the cart nears its final destination, you deal with one more onslaught, this one up close and personal. The cart continues through the mine exit, coming to rest at the radar installation and signaling the end of your mission.

UNDER THE RADAR

MISSION OBJECTIVES

- Find the Demolition Charges
- Disable Both Radar Stations
- Radio Allies Your Position
- Find Entrance to the HO-IX Hangar

WEAPONS

- Walther P-38
- B.A.R.
- Gewehr 43
- Bazooka
- Steil Grenades

FIND THE DEMOLITION CHARGES

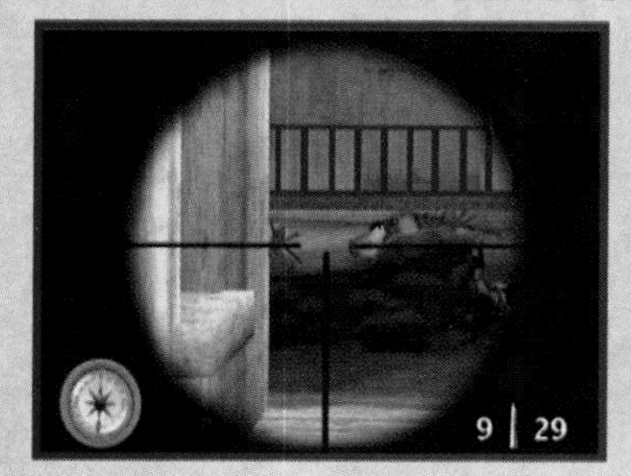

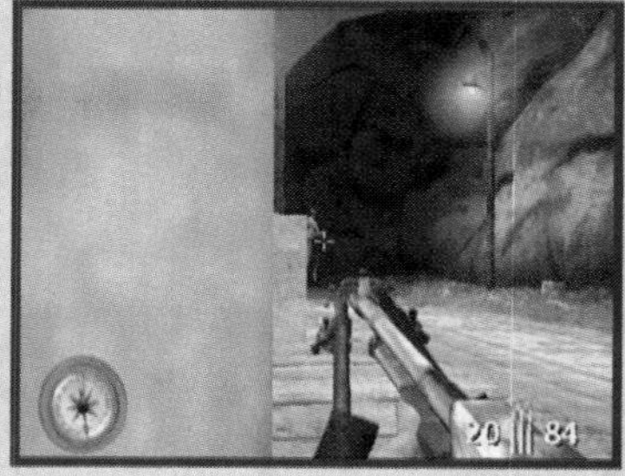

The mission begins in front of a shack, near the entrance to a German radar installation. Pick up the ammo on the porch, and edge out just far enough to eliminate the three-man machine-gun crew and another officer hiding around the corner. Run to the south side of the building to retrieve the Demolition Charges, but watch out for two more guards who show up.

DISABLE BOTH RADAR STATIONS

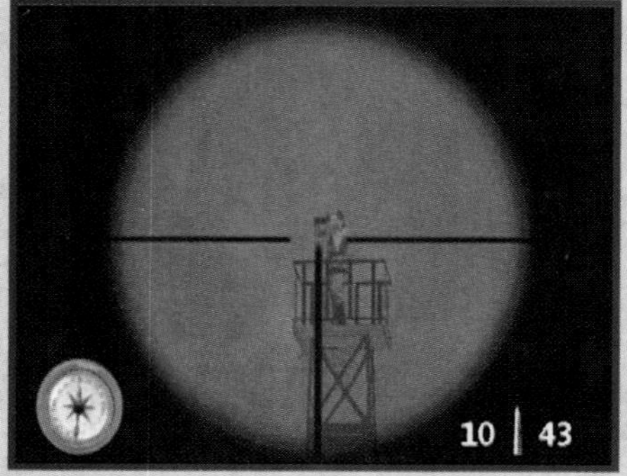

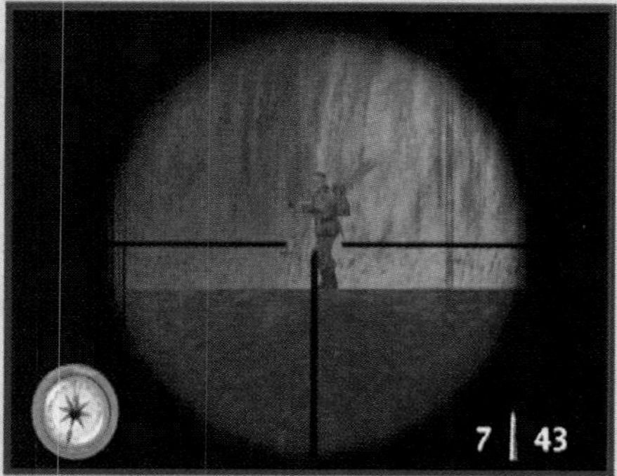

Your first radar station target is straight ahead. However, first you have some housecleaning to do. Sneak up to the railing on the right of the station. You have three critical targets: the sniper in the tower, a machine-gun nest to the left of the tower, and a Panzerschreck on the ledge above the machine gun. Watch for another gunner who takes over the machine gun after your initial attack. Do not reveal your position to the machine-gun nest, or the other attacks will be difficult to carry out. When the guns are silent, shoot the fuel drums near the truck to the right, just in case any enemies are around. If your health is slipping, pick up the Medical Kit alongside the fence to the right.

Run south to the radar tower, enter the building, and kill the guard inside. Set the Demolition Charge and exit the building. After the explosion, go back inside and drop down through the exploded floor grate.

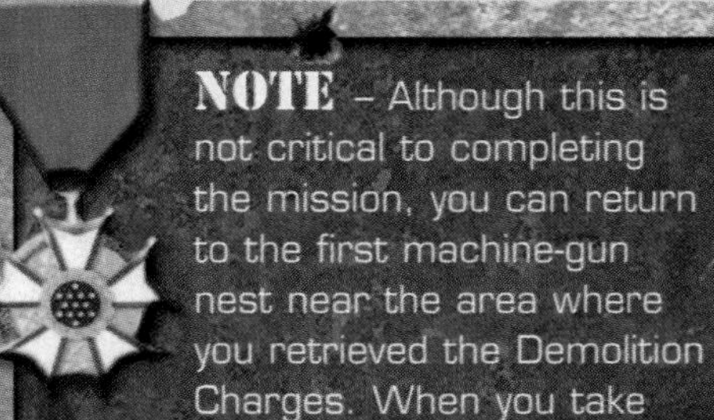

NOTE – Although this is not critical to completing the mission, you can return to the first machine-gun nest near the area where you retrieved the Demolition Charges. When you take over the gun, four soldiers appear at the end of the path (where you started the mission). They immediately begin shooting at you, so focus your line of fire on the soldiers as they arrive from the right. Clear the area, then go back and collect a Medical Kit, Medicinal Canteens, and ammo.

Edge carefully to the end of the tunnel—three guards are stacked to the right (the number may vary). Soften the attack or eliminate it completely by bouncing a few Steil Grenades off the wall. One of the soldiers may be armed with a Panzerschreck, so make sure to clear the area before you venture out into the yard.

You encounter one more soldier approaching from the right, behind the supply stack; don't rush out quite yet. Check the yard for ammo and health pickups. At the machine-gun nest, watch for activity on the north side of the yard. If you see one flash, more follow. Grab the machine gun and lay waste to any soldier foolish enough to rush you.

Walk to the southeast side of the runway and climb the ladder. Approach with caution because, depending on how quickly you arrive at this point, you could face heavy fire from the top of the ladder. At the top, enter a long winding path enclosed by cliffs that extend above head level. At the first fork, you have two choices. Go to the left to reach the backside of a shooting range. Four German soldiers shoot at you from the other side of a barbed-wire fence. The fire is intense, so do not stand there and exchange shots. Back up out of sight and lob a Grenade or two over the fence to wipe out the entire group. Now, return to the fork and continue down the right-hand path.

The right fork takes you to the front of the shooting range. If your foray to the left was successful, there's only one German soldier standing guard. Harvest the considerable cache of ammo, then exit the range to the south.

Work your way toward the southwest corner of the trenches. Danger lurks around every corner, so move carefully and keep your weapon loaded.

This mission's most difficult challenge begins. The winding trench reveals three structures ahead. Above the trench and to the left is the second radar installation. The machine-gun bunker below protects the installation and covers the path as it winds to the right. Finally, the third structure on the right is a ruined building that blocks access to the radar installation. There are several enemy soldiers here, along with a machine-gun nest.

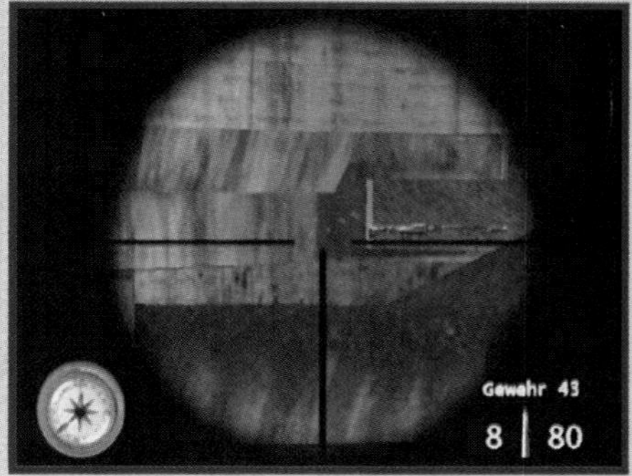

If you took out the gunners in the first bunker, keep walking along the path, but retrieve the Medical Kit below. Turn to the east to get a much better view of the radar installation and ruins. Another building at the end of the path on the left houses a single guard, a Field Surgeon Pack, and ammo.

From the time the first guard spots you in the trench, you come under heavy fire from the ruins and from the machine-gun nest above. When the area is clear, climb the steps, cross the plank to the other side, and turn left to go back toward the first machine-gun bunker.

Take the first right on the path that leads to the tower. The ladder is ahead; for now, focus your attention on the machine-gun bunkers to your left. If you cleaned out the bunkers earlier, jump inside, collect the ammo, and man the gun. Now, give a little back to the remaining guards in the ruins.

Climb the ladder to the tower and blow up the second radar installation. Walk around the catwalk to the doorway, take out the guard inside, and place your charge. On the catwalk, look to the northeast and take out the tower sniper.

RADIO ALLIES YOUR POSITION

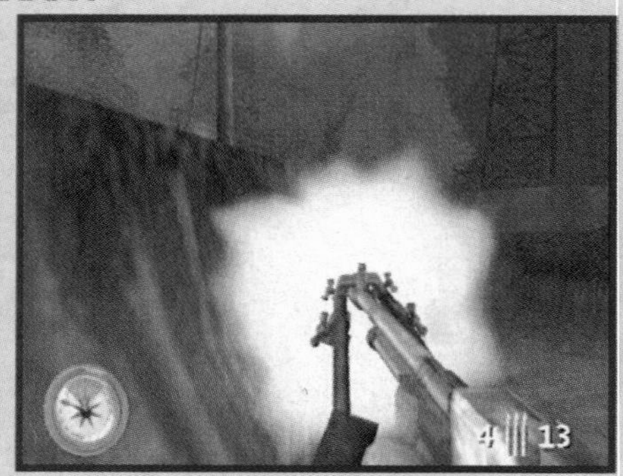

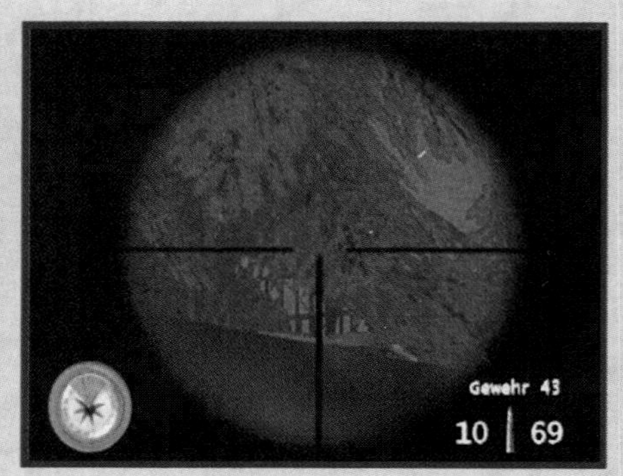

After the explosion, drop down through the floor and exit the installation to the north. Eliminate the German soldiers both on and above the path as you move toward the radio building. A sniper is almost completely hidden in the trees to the north (except for his boots).

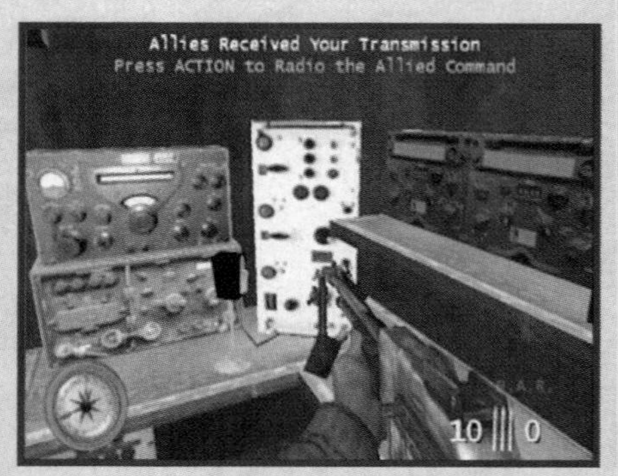

Dispatch the guard outside the radio building and walk inside. The radio operator is too busy to hear you, so he is an easy target. Step up to the radio and send your transmission.

FIND ENTRANCE TO THE HO-IX HANGAR

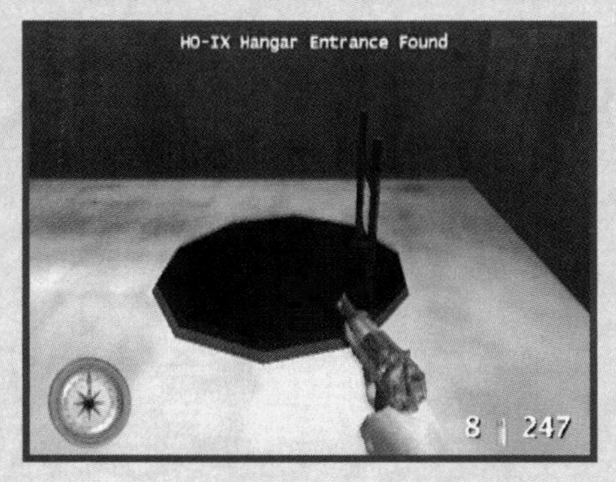

Move north to the next building, but watch out for the soldier hiding around the corner. Proceed down a narrow hallway to the hole in the floor. You've reached the access to the HO-IX hangar. Only one more mission to go!

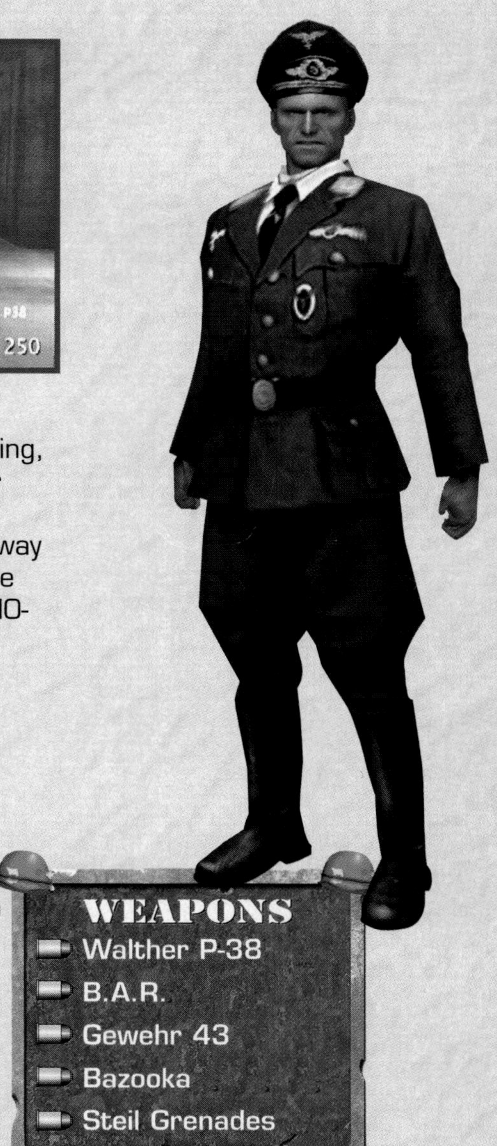

STEALING THE SHOW

MISSION OBJECTIVES

- Find and Eliminate Sturmgeist
- Steal the HO-IX

WEAPONS

- Walther P-38
- B.A.R.
- Gewehr 43
- Bazooka
- Steil Grenades

FIND AND ELIMINATE STURMGEIST

There's no warm-up time in this mission. As the curtain rises, Sturmgeist instructs every able-bodied soldier to devote himself to your destruction. You begin with a full complement of weapons. Carve a path through a sea of enemy soldiers to the hangar door east of your opening position. However, you can't run for it, and you don't have a wide enough range of fire to stay inside the bunker and select targets one at a time. The sheer number of enemies is tough enough, but the Panzerschrecks make this mission seem impossible.

Our strategy is simple to describe, but difficult to carry out. To best eliminate the hordes of German soldiers in front of you, bounce back and forth between the two machine-gun nests on either side of your bunker. When we say bounce, we mean it. Do not spend more than a few seconds at each gun. During the trips back and forth, grab much-needed health pickups. There are enough Medical Kits, Field Surgeon Packs, and Medicinal Canteens to keep you alive during the first few minutes—but only if you keep moving!

TIP – Watch your health carefully. When you exhaust the Field Surgeon Packs and Medical Kits in the immediate vicinity, go back into the bunker for six more Field Surgeon Packs. Be careful when you return, because the German soldiers will target the bunker and follow you to the door.

As the battle wears on, health becomes more critical, because you exhaust the Medical Kits and Field Surgeon Packs in the vicinity of the machine-gun nests. Pick your spots and race out to grab enough health to keep you going. Keep up the pace! There are fewer enemies on the battlefield, but the Panzerschreck is dangerous. Move around to present a more difficult target for the slow-firing rocket launchers. Pay special attention to the machine-gun nest on the other side of the battlefield. Don't linger in one nest too long if you are exchanging fire.

When the dust settles, scour the battlefield for ammo and health. You need bushels of B.A.R. ammo to take out Sturmgeist.

Shortly after you enter the hangar, Allied bombs collapse the roof, blocking your way to the next hangar. However, you can enter through the north door. Sturmgeist's henchmen are ready to intercept you when you enter the hangar, so load up and move cautiously.

After the shooting starts, retreat back into the first building for health pickups. Use your Gewehr and pick off the soldiers who follow you. If health is critical, run outside and pick up a Medicinal Canteen or two. When you return, break out your Bazooka or Grenades to finish off Sturmgeist's men. You only need the Gewehr or B.A.R. to take out the big guy, so don't hold back.

After eliminating Sturmgeist's soldiers, it's time for a showdown. You know Sturmgeist is alone when he launches a string of insults in your direction. Ignore the insults, but pay close attention to his very big gun. When you first approach the hangar, Sturmgeist hangs out around the covered pile of boxes. Toss a few Grenades in his direction to get him moving.

The Herr eventually sets up shop behind a wooden crate that is visible from the left side of the opening to the hangar. *Do not approach Sturmgeist from any other angle or he cuts you to pieces!* Edge over from the left until you see his blonde head; wait until he pops up. You take a hit or two while lining up the kill shot, but if your health is full going in, you have nothing to worry about.

STEAL THE HO-IX

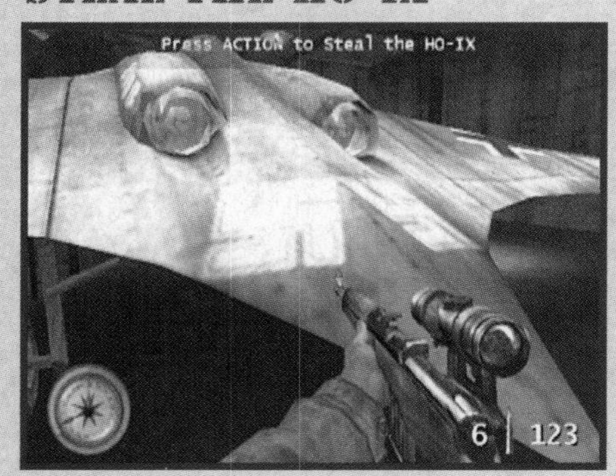

For the first time since D-Day, you can put your guns away! Walk up to the HO-IX, press the Action button and hop in the cockpit. You fly away from Gotha, victorious against Herr Sturmgeist and the German war machine. Enjoy the flight home; you earned it!

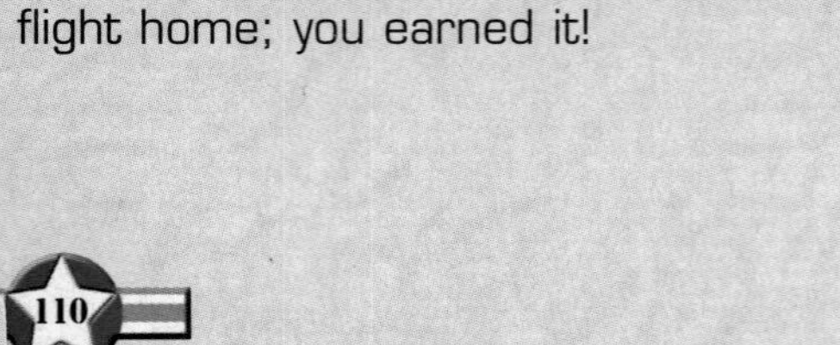